Enlightened Racism

CULTURAL STUDIES

Series Editors
Janice Radway, Duke University
Richard Johnson, University of Birmingham

Enlightened Racism: **The Cosby Show,**
Audiences, and the Myth of the American Dream
Sut Jhally and Justin Lewis

FORTHCOMING

Dreaming Identities: Class, Gender, and Generation
in 1980s Hollywood Movies Elizabeth G. Traube

The Madonna Connection: Representational Politics,
Subcultural Identities, and Cultural Theory
edited by Cathy Schwichtenberg

Reconceptualizing Audiences
edited by Jon Cruz and Justin Lewis

Frameworks of Culture and Power: Complexity and Politics
in Cultural Studies Richard Johnson

An Introduction to Media Studies
edited by Stuart Ewen, Elizabeth Ewen,
Serafina Bathrick, and Andrew Mattson

Art and the Committed Eye: Culture, Society, and
the Functions of Imagery Richard Leppert

ENLIGHTENED RACISM

The Cosby Show, Audiences,
and the Myth
of the American Dream

Sut Jhally
and Justin Lewis

WESTVIEW PRESS
Boulder • San Francisco • Oxford

Cultural Studies

Copyright © 1992 by Westview Press, Inc.

Published in 1992 in the United States of America by Westview Press, Inc., 5500 Central Avenue, Boulder, Colorado 80301-2847, and in the United Kingdom by Westview Press, 36 Lonsdale Road, Summertown, Oxford OX2 7EW

Library of Congress Cataloging-in-Publication Data
Jhally, Sut.
   Enlightened racism : The Cosby show, audiences, and the myth of
the American dream / Sut Jhally and Justin Lewis.
      p.   cm. — (Cultural studies)
   Includes bibliographical references and index.
   ISBN 0-8133-1418-6 — ISBN 0-8133-1419-4 (pbk.)
   1. Cosby show (Television program).   2. Afro-Americans in
television.   3. Television broadcasting—United States—Influence.
4. Television viewers—United States.   5. United States—Race
relations—Public opinion.   6. Public opinion—United States.
I. Lewis, Justin, 1958–   II. Title.   III. Series.
PN1992.77.C68J4   1992
791.45′72—dc20
                                                                    92-3836
                                                                    CIP

Printed and bound in the United States of America

10   9   8   7   6   5   4   3   2

"The country's image of the Negro, which hasn't very much to do with the Negro, has never failed to reflect with a kind of frightening accuracy the state of mind of the country."

—*James Baldwin*

"I believe that there will ultimately be a clash between the oppressed and those who do the oppressing. I believe that there will be a clash between those who want freedom, justice and equality for everyone and those who want to continue the system of exploitation. I believe that there will be that kind of clash, but I don't think it will be based on the color of the skin. . . ."

—*Malcolm X*

Contents

Rethinking Stereotypes, 138
Moving Beyond the American Dream, 139

Tables

Preface

This book deals with issues of immense political importance. It addresses two critical aspects of our contemporary culture: how our most ubiquitous cultural form, television, influences the way we think; and how American society thinks about race in the post–Civil Rights era. We chose to study audience reactions to *The Cosby Show* because of its position in relation to these two issues.

Already these issues have been the focus of much public debate. We intend this book to contribute to this debate, which we feel has become conceptually limited.

The argument of this book is fairly straightforward; yet it contains a few complexities informed by a range of academic traditions. For the sake of clarity and brevity, we have minimized our discussions of the theoretical aspects of our inquiry (which many academics, including ourselves, find interesting in their own right). Because we did not want the reader to get bogged down in theoretical abstractions or scholarly citations, we have kept these to a minimum. Although we have cited only a few selective works, we gratefully acknowledge the influence of those scholars working in the fields of media studies, audience research, and critical cultural studies. For those readers who would like more information concerning these academic areas and how they pertain to studies of this kind, *The Ideological Octopus: Explorations into Television and Its Audience* by Justin Lewis provides a useful introduction.

Sut Jhally
Justin Lewis

Acknowledgments

Our greatest debt is to Bill and Camille Cosby, who financed the empirical audience study on which much of this book is based. As the reader will realize from our conclusions, this funding came with no strings attached. We are grateful to the Cosbys for their open-mindedness and their commitment to scholarship and education.

We thank Betsey Chadwick, Glynda Christian, Leslye Colvin, Rob Dinozzi, Ernest Green, and Harold Schlechtweg, who made up the research team during the interview and coding stages of the project, and Elaine Stockwell, who transcribed many of the interviews. And we are grateful to Joseph Duffey and W. Barnett Pearce for their help and support and to George Gerbner, who generously made data from the Annenberg School's Cultural Indicators Project available to us.

S. J.
J. L.

1

Introducing
The Cosby Show

Neither *The Cosby Show* nor its star, Bill Cosby, need much introduction. By the early 1980s, Bill Cosby—stand-up comedian, actor (most re-membered for his costar role in the 1960s *I Spy* TV series), voice behind *Fat Albert,* and star of TV commercials—had established a modest and respectable place in the history of North American popular culture. It was, however, *The Cosby Show* that allowed Cosby to move from celebrity to superstardom. Whether one measures success in terms of wealth, fame, popularity, or respect, Bill Cosby is now undoubtedly among the most successful entertainers in the United States.

When it began in 1984, *The Cosby Show* did not look like a surefire hit. Its all-black cast offered viewers a gentle comedy without gimmicks, zany situations, or intriguing plot lines. Yet *The Cosby Show* has become the most successful TV show in recent history, the pinnacle of Cosby's long career. It topped the annual ratings lists year after year in the second half of the 1980s, and, although it has been displaced from the number one spot in the 1990s, it retains an enduring place in the world of prime-time television.

For those who have managed to avoid seeing it, *The Cosby Show* is a half-hour situation comedy about an upper middle class black family, the Huxtables. Cliff Huxtable (played by Bill Cosby) is a gynecologist and obstetrician, and his wife, Clair, is a lawyer. They have four daughters and a son; as the series has grown older, they have acquired in-laws and grandchildren. The Huxtables' attractive New York brownstone home is the setting for an endless series of comic domestic dramas. There is little in this description to distinguish this TV fiction from many others: we are used to a TV world populated by attractive professionals and their

1

good-looking offspring. What makes the show unusual is its popularity, its critical acclaim, and the fact that all its leading characters are black.

These distinctive achievements and features have made *The Cosby Show* the subject of much speculation. At the heart of much of the discussion lies an apparent contradiction. The United States is a country that is still emerging from a deeply racist history, a society in which many white people have treated (and continue to treat) black people with contempt, suspicion, and a profoundly ignorant sense of superiority. Yet the most popular U.S. TV show, among black and white people alike, is not only about a black family but a family portrayed without any of the demeaning stereotypical images of black people common in mainstream popular culture. Commentators have been provoked to try to resolve this apparent paradox and, in so doing, to ask themselves about the show's social significance.

The most prevalent critical reaction, particularly during the first few years of the show, was to applaud Bill Cosby's creation as not only a witty and thoughtful sitcom but also an enlightened step forward in race relations. After decades of degrading media images of black people in other shows, the Huxtable family presented black characters that black *and* white audiences could relate to. In this sense, the show was conceived in contrast to the stereotypical shows that preceded it. Psychiatrist Alvin Poussaint, an adviser to *The Cosby Show,* is highly critical of the black sitcoms of the 1970s—shows like *The Jeffersons, Sanford and Son,* and *Good Times,* which are, argues Poussaint "full of jivin', jammin', streetwise style stuff that is the worst kind of stereotyping" (quoted in Hartsough, 1989).

The Cosby Show, however, portrays comedic black characters with dignity and humanity. On a TV celebration of African-American comedy (*A Laugh, a Tear*), actor Tim Reid praised the show as "a breath of fresh air," showing, at last, "the reality of what was good about our neighborhoods . . . a reality of what was good about a black childhood." Here was a show that not only overcame traditional stereotypes but, in so doing, was both funny and incredibly popular. The celebratory tone of many reviews contained genuine hopes for what such a cultural intervention might achieve in dispelling racial prejudice in the United States.

The history of critical response to popular culture often follows a similar pattern: elaborate praise becomes an increasingly difficult burden, and critics' euphoria is almost invariably followed by cynical backlash. *The Cosby Show,* for good or ill, is no exception to this rule. Critics have begun to accuse the show of presenting a misleadingly cozy picture, a sugar candy world unfettered by racism, crime, and economic deprivation. Some have argued that the Huxtables' charmed life is so alien to the experience of most black people that they are no longer "black" at all but, as Henry Louis Gates (1989: 40) puts it, "in most respects, just like white people."

Gates's argument is not simply about whether *The Cosby Show* is "realistic"; he is also concerned about the show's effect on its enormous viewing audience. The crux of his case is that these "positive images" can actually be counterproductive because they reinforce the myth of the American dream, a just world where anyone can make it and racial barriers no longer exist:

> As long as *all* blacks were represented in demeaning or peripheral roles, it was possible to believe that American racism was, as it were, indiscriminate. The social vision of "Cosby," however, reflecting the miniscule integration of blacks into the upper middle class, reassuringly throws the blame for black poverty back onto the impoverished (Gates, 1989: 40).

At the risk of simplifying critical opinion, most analyses of *The Cosby Show* fit broadly into one of two views: the show is seen either as socially progressive or as an apology for a racist system that disadvantages most black people. Both views carry with them assumptions about media effects. The debate, therefore, concerns the nature of the show's social effect and raises questions that we hope to resolve in the following chapters about the meaning of the show for black and white audiences. But first it is useful to dwell a little longer on the issues that have earned the show both praise and condemnation.

COSBY: THE CASE FOR

If we are to do battle over the nature of what gets shown on prime-time television in the United States, we should be well versed in the art of the possible. Any attempt to change the form or content of mainstream television will come up against two powerful bastions of conservatism: the profit-oriented predilections of network and advertising executives, and the expectations and tastes of well-conditioned TV audiences. We can exhaust ourselves creating innovative programming ideas, but if the networks, advertisers, or viewers don't respond, then we are wasting our time.

The Cosby Show's focus on a black family and departure from accepted racial stereotypes did not make the series an obvious candidate for prime time. ABC turned the series proposal down. Without Bill Cosby's track record (including, significantly, his ability to sell products on TV commercials), the series would probably never have made it onto the air. To attack the show because it panders to the needs of a mainstream white audience is to attack its lifeblood: in the TV culture of the United States, audience ratings determine whether a series lives or dies. This bottom line gives a TV program very little room to maneuver. To have confronted the audience with the uncomfortable realities of racism would have been commercial suicide.

John Downing (1988: 68) argues that any evaluation of the show must take account of this conservative cultural climate, and that, despite its limitations, "to be as good as it is *and* to have gotten past these barriers is a major achievement in itself." Ultimately, Downing acknowledges, the show does let "racism off the hook." It is, nevertheless, a considerable step forward in the history of media representation. There is, Downing (1988: 61) argues, "an abundance of black culture presented in the series, expressed without fanfare, but with constant dignity." The show celebrates black artists, from Ellis Wilson to Stevie Wonder, and political figures like Martin Luther King, Jr., and events like the Civil Rights march on Washington have been interwoven, albeit ever so gently, into the story line.

The naming of the Huxtables' first grandchildren is a typical example of *The Cosby Show*'s quiet style. Their eldest daughter, Sondra, decides to call her twins Nelson and Winnie. The episode that deals with this decision highlights the issue of naming but makes no comment on the chosen names' overt political connotations. The reference to the Mandelas is made quietly and unobtrusively, relying upon the audience's ability to catch the political ramifications of the statement.

If such subtlety is a virtue, it was one born of necessity. During the show's second season, NBC tried to have the anti-apartheid sign on Theo's bedroom door removed. Bill Cosby, empowered by the newly achieved high ratings, successfully stood his ground to keep the sign. What is interesting about this event is not only Cosby's triumph (would the network have capitulated to a show receiving a few less ratings points?), but the almost pathological fear of certain kinds of political discourse by executives in charge of TV entertainment. The fuss was made about a sign expressing a sentiment that is, outside the comparatively small TV market of white South Africa, *supposed* to be fairly uncontroversial. The anti-apartheid sign made no intrusion into the plot, and many viewers probably did not even notice it. The network's desire to remove such a meek symbol of black resistance from the airwaves demonstrates what progressive voices on prime-time television are up against.

The seriousness with which *The Cosby Show* approaches the issue of cultural representation has invited critical scrutiny of the series. As Bill Cosby and program consultant Alvin Poussaint point out, few other sitcoms are attacked for their failure to deal with issues of racism. This is, Poussaint argues, a particularly unfair constraint to put upon a situation comedy. Writing in *Ebony,* Poussaint (quoted in Hartsough, 1989) points out that

> audiences tune in to be entertained, not to be confronted with social problems. Critical social disorders, like racism, violence, and drug abuse, rarely lend themselves to comic treatment; trying to deal with them on a sitcom could trivialize issues that deserve serious, thoughtful treatment.

The limits of *The Cosby Show,* are, according to Poussaint, the limits of the genre. This is a point, indeed, acknowledged by some critics. Gates (1989: 40) in an otherwise fairly critical piece, accepts that the very structure of a sitcom "militates against its use as an agent of social change."

Despite these constraints, what *The Cosby Show* has confronted, many have argued, is the deep-rooted racism of white Americans who find it difficult to accept racial equality. Michael Dyson (1989: 29), for example, has suggested that one of "the most useful aspects of Cosby's dismantling of racial mythology and stereotyping is that it has permitted America to view black folk as *human beings.*" Here, at last, are media representations of successful and attractive black people whom white people can respect, admire, and even identify with.

It could be argued that references to discrimination and black struggle would, in this sense, be counterproductive, alienating substantial sections of the white audience and making identification with the Huxtables more difficult. We should also be aware of the particular nature of the TV world. The Huxtables' class position may be unusual in real life (for black *and* white people), but to be an affluent, attractive professional on television is to be normal. This argument makes assumptions, of course, about the audience, just as do the arguments of persons critical of the show's lack of discourse on racial discrimination.

Some of the more positive evaluations of the show have made this interesting point: the discourse of discrimination that does find its way into the script is not about racism but sexism. The show frequently uses humor to expose the inadequacy of the sexist or machismo attitudes of some members of its male cast. Some characters, like son-in-law Elvin or Rudy's friend Kenny (who spouts the sexist platitudes of his big brother), are deliberately set up to be undermined. Although it is Clair and her daughters who take the lead in these instances, they are usually supported by Cliff, who has traveled some way beyond the sexist male stereotype so common in TV sitcoms.

It is unusual to find strong male characters in sitcoms who support a feminist stance taken by female characters. The male in a sitcom who adopts such a position invariably still risks ridicule. Downing (1989:

60) suggests that, although *The Cosby Show*'s challenge to patriarchy has its limitations, Cliff's involvement in these comic episodes plays an important role in legitimating the show's feminist sentiments: "His condemnation of everyday sexism perhaps communicates itself all the more powerfully to male viewers precisely because he cannot be written off as a henpecked wimp."

Downing's defense of *The Cosby Show* is not apologetic: it is a reminder that, however we judge it, the show is, in many respects, one of the more progressive forces in popular culture to emerge from the United States in recent years. This may not be saying very much—we are, after all, talking about a televisual history steeped in sexist and racist images— but it is worth remembering before we embark on a journey to scrutinize the North American audience. Even if the audience study confirms many of the critics' worst fears about *The Cosby Show*'s contributions to racism, there are countless other TV messages whose ideological consequences are almost too oppressive or frightening even to contemplate.

COSBY: THE CASE AGAINST

Few would argue that *The Cosby Show* presents a realistic view of the lives and experiences of typical black Americans. The Huxtable family, like its creator, has attained a level of wealth, comfort, and success shared by only a tiny minority of black people in the United States. The period that produced *The Cosby Show* has also produced, the show's critics argue, a deterioration in the social conditions of most black Americans.

The success of *The Cosby Show,* according to Gates, has led to a curious divergence between media images and social realities. Bill Cosby has broken the mold of black media stereotypes and opened up our TV screens to a host of black performers:

> This is the "Cosby" decade. The show's unprecedented success in depicting the lives of affluent blacks has exercised a profound influence on television in the last half of the 80's . . . "Cosby's" success has led to the flow of TV sitcoms that feature the black middle class, each of which takes its lead from the "Cosby" show (Gates, 1989: 1).

Yet, outside the world of television, there are abundant social statistics to demonstrate that many of the advances made by black Americans in the 1960s and 1970s are being reversed in the 1980s and 1990s, so that, as Gates (1989: 40) puts it, "There is very little connection between the social status of black Americans and the fabricated images of black people that Americans consume every day." This argument is an important one. It relies upon specific claims about the nature of the worlds within and outside television and places *The Cosby Show* in the context of a more general argument about representation and reality. We shall, with the aid of social statistics and our own content analysis, consider its validity in more detail in Chapter 4.

The gulf between television and the world outside is, some have argued, propounded by the Huxtables' charmed lives, a utopian familial harmony that has caused some critics to wince in disbelief. Mark Crispin Miller's (1986: 206) description is characteristically derisive:

> And then there is the cuddliest and most beloved of TV Dads: Bill Cosby, who, as Dr. Heathcliff Huxtable, lives in perfect peace, and in a perfect brownstone, with his big happy family, and never has to raise his hand or fist, but retains the absolute devotion of his wife and kids just by making lots of goofy faces.

The problem that Gates and Miller are identifying is not simply that the show is an unrealistic portrayal of black family life (few sitcoms, after all, make any claim to represent social reality) but that the Huxtables sustain the harmful myth of social mobility.

The Huxtable family appears to have glided effortlessly into the upper echelons of American middle class society. The show never offers us the slightest glimpse of the economic disadvantages and deep-rooted discrimination that prevent most black Americans from reaching their potential. Michael Dyson (1989: 30), in an otherwise positive assessment of the show, makes this comment:

> It is perhaps this lack of acknowledgement of the underside of the American Dream that is the most unfortunate feature of the Huxtable opulence. Cosby defends against linking the authenticity of the Huxtable representation of black life to the apparently contradictory luxury the family lives in when he says: "To say that they are not black enough is a denial of the American Dream and the American way of life. My point is that this is an American family—an *American* family—and if you want to live like they do, and you're willing to work, the opportunity is there."

But, as Dyson suggests, this is a cruel distortion: "Such a statement leads us to believe that Cosby is unaware that there are millions of people, the so-called working poor, who work hard but nevertheless fall beneath the poverty level." And yet, writes Dyson, "surely Cosby knows better than this."

Whatever Bill Cosby's intention, some critics argue that the result is extremely damaging. The Huxtables' achievements ultimately lend credibility to the idea that "anyone can make it," the comforting assumption of the American dream, which is a myth that sustains a conservative political ideology blind to the inequalities hindering persons born on mean streets and privileging persons born on easy street. As Miller (1986: 210) puts it, "Cliff's blackness serves an affirmative purpose within the ad that is *The Cosby Show*. At the center of this ample tableau, Cliff is himself an ad, implicitly proclaiming the fairness of the American system: 'Look!' he shows us. 'Even *I* can have all this!'" This mythology is made all the more powerful, Miller argues, by the close identification between Cliff Huxtable and Bill Cosby. Behind the fictional doctor lies a man whose real life is *also* a success story: fact and fiction here coalesce to confirm the "truth" they represent.

Herein, the critics argue, lies the popularity of the show in the United States. The show may appear to herald a new dawn of racial tolerance, a world in which white people accept black people into their living rooms as equals. This appearance, according to Miller, hides the more subtle fears of white viewers, to whom black people still seem threatening. Cliff, or Bill Cosby, is attractive to white viewers because, as Miller (1986: 213–214) puts it, he represents "a threat contained," offering "deep solace to a white public terrified that one day blacks might come with guns to steal the copperware, the juicer, the microwave, the VCR, even the TV itself" and at a time when "American whites need such reassurance because they are now further removed than ever, both spatially and psychologically, from the masses of the black poor."

Despite Miller's hyperbole, the thrust of this argument may provide us with an insight into the ideological state of white people in the contemporary United States. *The Cosby Show* is not simply a source of gentle reassurance; it flatters to deceive. The United States is still emerging from a system of apartheid. Even if legal and political inequalities are finally disappearing, economic barriers remain. In an age when most white people have moved beyond the crudities of overt and naked racism, there is a heavy burden of guilt for all concerned. *The Cosby Show* provides its white audience with relief not only from fear but also from responsibility.

ASKING THE AUDIENCE

How well do these differing assessments explain the show's popularity and significance? More than any other, this question motivated us to go beyond conjecture and seek the answer from the show's viewers, about whom both arguments make assumptions. Accordingly, we designed and carried out a major qualitative audience study not only of opinions about *The Cosby Show* but also of attitudes toward the issues raised by commentators and critics.

vacillate between the wisdom of fatherhood and a childlike, comic self-mockery; their son, Theo, is the good-natured but typical male adolescent, full of bravado and misconceptions (for his parents to put right); and the two youngest daughters, Vanessa and Rudy, are both cute and mischievous.

The Huxtables are an upper middle class black family, and one of the study's aims was to explore how audiences interpret images and issues of race and class. These issues are explicitly raised in the show only rarely, although they are both alluded to very gently. References to black culture and black history, for example, are invariably apolitical. In this episode, we are reminded that the Huxtables are African Americans by the presence of a visiting friend from Trinidad, Dr. Harman. During the show, Cliff teases his friend about his accent, symbolizing both the unities and differences between the two black cultures. The presence of another doctor also emphasizes the Huxtables' own class position: here we are seeing professionals mixing with other professionals.

For viewers familiar with *The Cosby Show,* any episode carries with it a multitude of allusions and references to other shows. Although respondents were asked in the interview to address this episode specifically, they were also encouraged to talk about *The Cosby Show* more generally.

In the interviews we wanted the discussion to flow freely. The questions were quite open-ended, particularly during the first part of the interview, to allow respondents the freedom to set their own agenda. Respondents were first asked simply to describe the story they felt they had just been told. Then they were asked a series of general questions to stimulate conversation, questions like, "What do you think this episode was about?" and "What do you think of Clair Huxtable?"

These innocuous questions often succeeded in opening up the discussion by giving respondents the opportunity to remark on attitudes toward class, race, or gender, attitudes the interviewer could then explore. If respondents were less forthcoming, the interviewer would ask them to comment on these topics—for example, "How would you feel if the Huxtable family were white?" and "Would the show be as good if the Huxtables were a blue-collar family?" Because the initial responses to these questions were sometimes ambiguous, guarded, or even misleading, the answers were carefully explored in the ensuing discussion.

The subject that provoked the most cautious or evasive reactions (among white groups particularly) was race. In order to ease the discomfort people might feel in addressing this issue, white groups were interviewed by white interviewers and black groups by black interviewers, a strategy that was clearly validated when we analyzed the transcripts. Attitudes to race were also approached from two different angles: first, in relation to *The Cosby Show*; and second, toward the end of the interview, in

The results of this study, as we shall demonstrate, are extremely revealing. We find that they enable us not only to clarify and develop the debate about *The Cosby Show* but also to comment more generally upon the whole issue of stereotyping on television.

At an early stage, we realized that whatever an audience study might reveal about these arguments, it would lead beyond the usual limits of TV audience research. It is impossible to design an audience study that, in a simple and straightforward sense, measures the effect of the series on attitudes toward race. Such an issue cannot be resolved from the responses to simple multiple-choice questions. An exploration of the show's influence forces us to delve into the complex interaction between the program and the viewer. From that point, we can look into the delicate ideological suppositions that inform the sites where program and viewer meet to create meaning and pleasure.

Our approach was modeled on recent qualitative audience studies from within what can be broadly termed a cultural studies tradition. We assume that the significance, or meaning, of television in popular culture is a product of the interplay between a television program and the attitudes the viewer brings to it. We accept, therefore, that television is influential. But we also accept that the precise nature of its influence is unpredictable: it will depend upon viewers who have thoughts, interests, and opinions before they sit down in front of the screen.

Research of this kind is, nevertheless, easier said than done. Establishing connections between attitudes and perceptions is technically difficult and demanding. It is a little like a trial in which the jury can only reconstruct events from evidence and testimony presented to it after the fact. So it is with this kind of investigative audience research inasmuch as we cannot perch inside people's brains and watch ideas and opinions forming. Like the prudent jury, we must use our knowledge and skill to interpret what people tell us rather than accept all testimony at face value.

This must necessarily be a painstaking procedure, and we will not try the reader's patience by detailing it completely. Suffice to say that we decided to carry out a number of in-depth discussions with people about not only the show but also the issues that we felt might be relevant to their understanding of it. Each discussion was recorded and transcribed, providing us with voluminous data to be analyzed and interpreted.

Our respondents came from Springfield in western Massachusetts. In many respects, Springfield is a fairly typical small North American city. It has rich neighborhoods and poor neighborhoods. It has housing projects and leafy suburbs. It is, like the United States, racially mixed: predominantly white, but with prominent black and Hispanic populations (particularly in the poorer neighborhoods near the city center). Its "ordinariness" indeed, was commented upon by journalist Bill Moyers, who in 1990 chose Springfield as the venue for a TV program because he felt it was a microcosm of national attitudes and opinions.

We structured the selection of participants so as to test certain variables that might influence viewers' interpretations of the show: in particular, race, class, and gender. We then organized the people we interviewed into 52 small focus groups (a large sample for a qualitative study): 23 black, 3 Hispanic, and 26 white. The black and white interviewees were subdivided by social class (using standard socioeconomic occupational categories). Most groups included men and women, although there were some groups of all men or all women. The only requirement that all interviewees met was that they were either frequent or occasional viewers of *The Cosby Show* (a qualification that, in the United States, is inclusive rather than exclusive).

Focus group interviews usually involve bringing together people who have certain things in common (age, social class, gender, interests) to generate a structured conversation around certain topics. The conversations that ensue, we have found, are usually slightly formal among people who may not feel entirely at ease with one another. Many are shy about expressing their thoughts and opinions in such a contrived situation. Because we meant to delve into some often sensitive areas (such as attitudes about race, gender, and class), we were keen to create a comfortable atmosphere for the focus groups.

To encourage a relaxed air of easy informality, we conducted all the interviews in people's homes in groups of two to six people who knew one another well. The groups were made up of families and/or friends; our main requirement was that group members should be close to one another and feel comfortable about watching television together. In an informal setting, conversation could be allowed at appropriate moments to flow freely without interruption by the interviewer.

Each interview began with the interviewer and the group sitting down together to watch a video recording of an episode of *The Cosby Show*. Apart from being an obvious way to begin a discussion based on the program, this experience created, from the outset, a certain amount of common ground between the interviewer and the respondents. The interviewer could then use the show as a reference point for the exploration of issues and ideas.

The episode chosen for the viewing/interview sessions was fairly typical in a number of respects (a synopsis of the episode appears at the end of this chapter). It develops two interweaving narratives and resolves them in the style of a gentle moral tale. The issue dealt with in this episode, as in many others, is sexism, and the main characters strike familiar attitudes. Clair Huxtable is a figure of moral authority; her husband, Cliff, the key player in the episode's comedy, is allowed to that she gave him no warning that Lindy had become a beautiful woman; had he known, he would have dressed for the occasion. Clair scolds him and makes fun of his sexist attitude.

Scene 4: After Dinner, the Living Room

The families enter the living room. The two men immediately try to escape to the backyard. Theo makes clumsy (and slightly comic) efforts to impress Lindy, for which his sisters Vanessa and Rudy tease him. Lindy offers to show Theo more information about Outward Bound, and they exit (to the taunts of Vanessa and Rudy). The men finally escape to the backyard to play pétanque.

Commercial Break

Scene 5: The Backyard

The two men prepare for their game, bantering in a parody of competitive machismo. Even though the temperature is below freezing, both men display bravado by stripping down to their shirts.

Scene 6: The Living Room

The two women are playing cards. Lindy is telling Theo about her interest in rock climbing (part of her Outward Bound trip), a subject in which Theo suddenly declares a long-standing interest. Clair teases him, speculating on his subscription to *Rock and Woman*. Theo takes Lindy into the basement so that she can teach him about rock climbing.

Scene 7: The Basement

While Lindy tries to teach Theo some basic rock-climbing techniques, Theo tries to turn on the charm. Theo decides, against Lindy's protest, to show off by climbing the side of the basement staircase.

Scene 8: The Backyard

The final and deciding game. After more competitive (and comic) banter, the last balls are thrown. Both fall at about the same distance from the target ball, leading to a dispute about who has won. The two men go indoors to ask their wives to decide which ball is nearer.

Scene 9: The Living Room

The two women are reading magazines. Their husbands enter and ask them to resolve the dispute. Clair responds by making fun of their childish predicament. A crash is heard from the basement; all four go to investigate.

Scene 10: The Basement

Theo has fallen down the stairs, having attempted to do a handstand on the banister. Drs. Harman and Huxtable use the occasion to joke about each other's medical ability (to attend to Theo).

Scene 11: The Living Room

The two women are looking out of the front door. Theo enters and Clair describes the scene to him: the Harmans' car would not start, and both men's attempts to fix it succeed only in dismantling the engine. Lindy, a student of car maintenance, steps in to help them out. This, Clair tells Theo with a smile, is where women should be: under the hood rather than draped across it. The men are left "sitting on the curb."

2

Television and Reality: How Real Is *The Cosby Show*?

One notion, perhaps more than any other, limits our understanding of television's influence: the idea that we are *rational beings,* incapable of holding two contradictory ideas in our heads at the same time. It is an attractive notion. If we accept it, the world becomes a logical and straightforward place, inhabited by people with definable and coherent attitudes. If a social scientist wants to find out how people think, all he or she needs to do is ask them.

If only it were that simple. Unfortunately, the more we investigate something as imprecise as attitude and opinion, the murkier things become. Attitudes are slippery, ill-disciplined creatures; they can slide around our brains without our ever pausing to reflect upon their mutual compatibility. We are able, in other words, to think in entirely contradictory and illogical ways. We can, for example, be aware that commercials seek to manipulate us but still be seduced by them. We may be skeptical about a political candidate's promise not to raise taxes but nevertheless vote for them partly on the strength of that promise: in polls following the 1988 presidential race, voters indicated that they did not believe George Bush when he promised he would not raise taxes, but they wanted to elect someone who *seemed* to believe a promise that they thought he would not keep.

In a sophisticated world shaped by complex human achievements, how can we account for such commonplace lapses into irrationality? One answer is to look not so much at the *substance* of our thoughts but at their *form*.

Though attitudes can be based upon the logic of a series of propositions, they can also rest upon a much flimsier foundation. We can develop an attitude about a thing simply because we *associate* it with another thing.

15

We may choose a particular brand of soft drink, for instance, because we associate it with having a good time. In much the same way, we may feel good about our country because we associate it with a set of selective but positive images. These are not attitudes solidly constructed on reason; they are ideas built by association. This mode of thinking has been a prominent part of culture in the United States ever since the advertising industry discovered that appeals based upon association were much more effective than appeals based upon providing consumers with rational information about products.

Our ability to construct a consistent worldview depends upon linking these associations; otherwise our ideas may swim around disconnectedly like fish in an aquarium, drifting independently, never touching. In a world where we are exposed to thousands of messages every day from different sources (Coke, Pepsi, McDonalds, Levi's, Chevrolet, etc.), connecting the dots into some kind of coherence takes more time, effort, and thought than most of us can give. Accordingly, we can, and indeed do, hold two conflicting ideas in our minds without ever realizing it. Such thinking allowed many people to vote for Ronald Reagan (because he made them feel good about being "American") though they disagreed with many of his specific policies on matters of great importance.

A number of observers have become aware that television is not an innocent bystander in this matter. Television has become increasingly adept at using the language of association rather than the language of persuasion and argument. It is easier, now, to sell a product or a politician on television by constructing a simple association (breakfast cereals with the healthy people who eat them on commercials, politicians with the flags they surround themselves with on news appearances) than by developing an argument. The latter requires the viewer to pay attention— which, in an age of channel switching and instant gratification, most viewers are not inclined to do (and most TV producers know it).

Television's easy (easy to watch, easy to absorb) utilization of these discrete and separate messages creates not only superficiality but incoherence—it blurs the line between sense and nonsense. A detailed examination of attitudinal data suggests that the more television we watch, the more we are able to hold contradictory ideas simultaneously. Michael Morgan (1989: 250), following an exhaustive review of television viewing and survey data, offered this conclusion:

> Television cultivates a set of paradoxical currents. In a nutshell, heavy viewers think like conservatives, want like liberals, and yet call themselves moderates. They are less likely to vote but quicker to turn against an incumbent. They think elected officials don't care about what happens to them but are more interested in their personal lives than in their policies. They want to cut taxes

but improve education, medical care, social security. They distrust big government but want it to fix things for them, to protect them at home and from foreign threats. They praise freedom but want to restrict anyone who uses it in an unconventional way. They are losing confidence in people who run virtually all institutions, including religion, but they express trust in God, America—and television.

This is not stupidity or insanity; it is merely a response to the way television speaks to us, in a voice whose clarity is brief and discontinuous, with the ankle-deep profundity of unrelated epigrams.

At the heart of this televisual bounty of mixed messages is our ambivalence toward their reality. Many of us know that most television is fiction, yet we see television as a key source of information about the world we live in. It is simultaneously real *and* unreal. We may know, for example, that television exaggerates the scale of violent crime for dramatic purposes; nevertheless, studies show that the more television we watch, the more violent we assume the world to be. Our awareness of exaggeration, in other words, is only momentary.

This grants TV producers and program makers the enormous luxury of power without responsibility. They have the means to influence our view of the world without ever claiming to do so. Most television, goes the gigantic disclaimer, is (after all) nothing more than "entertainment." This grants television an insidious form of poetic license, apparently innocent because it is achieved with our complicity. Producers and consumers enter into a kind of conspiracy of cognitive dissonance, proposing two contradictory ideas at the same time without acknowledging the contradiction. This is an unwitting form of manipulation that occurs because we, as TV viewers, suspend our disbelief so automatically that we forget that we are in a state of suspension.

We shall, in this chapter, develop and illustrate this point with viewers' reactions to *The Cosby Show*. This is not an argument of merely passing interest: it implicates the whole process of watching television with having social significance. Television provides us with pictures of the world, of *our world,* and the knowledge that most of these pictures are fictional does not immunize us from believing in them. The beliefs we form become part of the context within which we understand who we are. To understand prime-time television, then, is to understand an important part of the way we view the world and ourselves.

TALKING ABOUT REALITY

One of the more curious aspects of our attitude toward television is that most of us feel far more able to comment on the merits of TV fiction than on news or current affairs. It is revealing to think about *how* people talk about different forms of television.

People will often charge the TV fictions that they dislike with being "unrealistic." Most qualitative audience studies are peppered with such remarks, praising or damning TV programs because they are or are not "real." Although many TV fictions strive for realism and can be subsequently held accountable, this is a criticism that could more appropriately be leveled at TV news. More than any other TV form, news purports to represent reality. We might, for example, accuse TV news in the United States of giving an unrealistic portrayal of Central America, or crime, or the president, or simply the world we live in—yet we prefer to criticize forms we know are fictional.

Why do we do this? Not simply because viewers assume unquestioningly that the news is "real." Most of us find it difficult to get close enough to the news to make any form of critical judgment. A detailed analysis of TV talk suggests that most people feel more able to evaluate TV fiction because it seems much closer to their own lives and the world they live in than does TV news. The worlds of soap operas and sitcoms are often worlds TV viewers can relate to—and if they can't, that becomes a direct ground for criticism. The contents of TV news, contrarily, often might almost be beamed in from another planet.

TV news, as a form of communication, is thus deeply flawed; but we are more concerned here with how it contrasts with TV fiction. Though the pictures of the world painted by news programs often seem remote, the visions conjured up by sitcoms, soaps, and drama series intrude far more intimately into our lives. As Ruth Rosen (1986: 46) has commented, it is fairly common for people to see characters on TV more often than they see members of their own family. These characters become part of our social milieu, people we can gossip about and discuss in the familiar terms that we use for friends or acquaintances. Further, the stronger our emotional investment in a character or situation, the harder it becomes to separate fantasy from reality. Actors and actresses who play characters in soap operas regularly report that they receive mail for their characters and that many people engage them in the everyday world as if they were that character. For actors and actresses playing the part of villains, this is not always a pleasant experience.

Television allows us to regularly invite a select group of people into our homes. Though most of these people are fictional characters, their regular visits create a sense of familiarity that is hard to resist. These visits are all the more pleasurable because the visitors are "real" enough to be incorporated into our lives. Even if we know, in the end, that these TV characters are too good to be true, we enjoy, in a very real sense, having them around. Some people in our study articulated that feeling fairly clearly:

> *The part of me that gets sucked into TV really wants to go over and have dinner with the Huxtable family, 'cause I feel like it's one of the few instances on TV where I've watched it on a regular basis, and feel something for the characters and kind of wish they were real people and someday bump into them, meet them.*

> *He's so likable, and I get the feeling if he were your neighbor or your relative, you'd love to see him come in. I do, anyway. I think he's just a real nice guy.*

Even when TV's characters are demonstrably different from anybody (anybody real, that is) we know, the familiarity may still remain. Elihu Katz and Tamar Liebes, in their cross-cultural study of audiences of *Dallas,* discovered that this response does not depend on our having economic or cultural characteristics in common with our televisual visitors. For example, regular *Dallas* viewers from outside the United States developed a "feeling of intimacy with the characters," and viewers' conversations about them have

> a "gossipy" quality which seems to facilitate an easy transition to discussion of oneself and one's close associates. It is likely that the continuous and indeterminate flow of the programme, from week to week, in the family salon invites viewers to invest themselves in fantasy, thought and discussion (Katz and Liebes, 1985: 32).

Once we allow ourselves this degree of familiarity, it is possible to see how fantasy and reality fade quietly into one another, how our TV friends and acquaintances take their place within our "real" world and jostle for attention and support with our "real" friends and family. This blurring of the distinction between fantasy and everyday life was a constant feature of nearly all our respondents' comments. Particular attention should be paid to the way in which people speak about characters on the show, not just to the specific content of their comments.

We found that many viewers were so engaged with the situations and the characters on television that they naturally read beyond the scene or program they were discussing and speculated about them as real events and characters. During discussions of the prehistory of the show, for example, Cliff and Clair's lives before their appearance on television are sketched out by viewers as if they were real people with real histories. One discussion among upper middle class white respondents focused on how Cliff must have taken care of the kids when Clair was going to law school. One female respondent remarked: "He had to have used babysitters. He had to have used babysitters." It did not matter that the prehistory was concocted by a scriptwriter to give some background. For this viewer, the situation *demanded* additional explanation.

Similarly, another (black) female respondent, while reconstructing for us the show she had just watched (which included a comic story told by Clair of a previous visit by their evening's guest that resulted in the next door neighbors calling in the police to sort out a quarrel over pétanque) remarked:

> *What was interesting was if the neighbors were white. . . . You always think of that, you know. At any rate, the police came, and you wondered if the police were white or black too, because they got right into the game.*

Once again, the realm of speculation goes well beyond the fictional confines of the script. This respondent's comments reveal quite a remarkable degree of engagement with the messages of television.

In a similar way, viewers would, without any prompting, speculate about the motivations of the characters. In the episode we showed our respondents, Theo's mother catches him looking at girly magazines that are thinly disguised as car magazines. Although some viewers found the ease with which he gave in to Clair unrealistic, one woman read it as a sign that he wanted to be discovered with them so he would be forced to remove them:

> RESPONDENT: *And I think he really wanted his mother to find that magazine.*

> INTERVIEWER: *Oh, why's that?*

> RESPONDENT: *No, I think so. You don't think so? I think it's kind of a boy's ploy because they um, I can see it with my kids at school. They will leave things around hoping that you will find it but not wanting to say please find it.*

> INTERVIEWER: *Why would he want her to find it?*

> RESPONDENT: *I don't know whether he was just going through that phase and . . . he didn't want to get rid of it because she said get rid of them, he did. . . .*

> INTERVIEWER: *Someone [in the interview group] made a comment like "Gee, he sure behaved."*

> RESPONDENT: *Yeah, that's what I'm saying.*

In this instance the viewer was intermingling her experiences as a schoolteacher with what she saw on her periodic visits to the Huxtable household and creating a complex web of motivations to explain Theo's behavior.

We also found that many viewers empathized to such a degree that they quite freely attributed flesh-and-blood feelings such as sympathy and jealousy to the characters. In the following case, a white middle class woman refers to a scene in another episode when a fellow student had planted a joint in Theo's book (later found by Cliff and Clair):

> *I felt sorry for Theo because having, you know, been in school [as a teacher] just up to a little over a year ago, I have seen that happen. Kids do that to each other, set each other up . . . or plant things to protect themselves. Not necessarily to set the other kid up, but just to protect themselves, sometimes. . . . So that really bothered me, to see poor Theo having that done to him.*

Discussions of relations between characters thus take on the tone in which one discusses one's friends and family. The following is a discussion between four of our respondents (three female and one teenage male) concerning the relation between Rudy and Olivia:

> F1: *Rudy to me now is getting sort of grown. She's different than when she first started out.*

> F2: *She's so different, mean. She's not the nice little girl she used to be. She's so mean to . . .*

> M1: *Rudy's not cute.*

> F2: *. . . to the little girl. Her . . .*

> F3: *The new little girl?*

> F2: *The new little girl.*

> M1: *She's cute.*

> F2: *She wants to be the boss.*

> F1: *. . . jealousy.*

> F2: *Yeah. The one with the ducks. She didn't want her playing with her little duck. And I thought she was too big to play with that duck anyway.*

> F1: *She's been the baby in the family all along.*

> F3: *Is this the grandchild? Who is that little child?*

F2: *Is that Elvin's?*

F3: *Oh, Lisa Bonet's.*

F1: *Lisa Bonet's daughter.*

F3: *Oh, okay.*

M1: *She's wonderful.*

F1: *The little girl. She's taking Rudy's place 'cause she's really good.*

F2: *I think maybe that's, you know . . . and then another baby comes along, and she's been the baby for so many years.*

F3: *Look how old she is. She's what, twelve? Eleven?*

The respondents are not only commenting on the fact that the youngest Huxtable daughter is not as cute as she used to be; they explain why this might be. Notice also that no one questions the blurring of the line between reality and fantasy. Lisa Bonet the actress is the mother of Olivia the character. There is no need to question this relationship because Lisa Bonet *is* Denise.

This blurring, this mixing of fantasy and reality, is always present in our engagement with the symbolic forms of our everyday lives. At its most straightforward, it can be expressed as a wish that everyday life were like television. A middle class black teenage female respondent commented on Clair Huxtable:

I think she's nice. She's patient. Sometimes I wish Ma would be patient. She's just a nice person. She's not mean, and she's patient, and she's a good wife and a good mother.

A young black couple, identifying themselves with the Huxtables' sense of loyalty and love, exhibited a similar sense of blurring in discussing the sexual infidelities of their friends. The wife commented:

We feel like fish out of water. It's . . . maybe we want to identify with the Huxtables. You know [with] that couple that they love each other, they stay home.

Thus the justification for their own lifestyle comes from another part of their significant reality, television. Cliff and Clair are part of a circle of friends with whom they can form an emotional attachment and alliances of identification against their other, real friends.

We are returned to television's central ambiguity: we know that these characters are not real, yet we gain pleasure from them in part because they *seem* real. Of course people know that Clair Huxtable is a fictional character enacted by Phylicia Rashad. They can distinguish between character and actress, especially if prompted to talk critically about a TV show; yet how Clair functions in terms of viewers' maps of the world is the same as if she were real. Television characters, especially those whom we recognize as realistic, become part of the framework within which we make sense of the world.

THE ABSENCE AND PRESENCE OF CLASS

An alien researching life on Earth would certainly learn a great deal by scrutinizing satellite broadcasts of television from the United States. The inquiring alien might, nevertheless, ponder various curiosities: Who collects the garbage or cleans the streets? Who builds the houses, farms the land, or works on production lines to produce all those delightful gadgets? Strangest of all, How does the economy sustain all those lawyers and doctors, who seem to be everywhere? This planet, the alien might conclude, is chronically overpopulated by members of the middle and upper middle classes.

These curiosities are, in a different way, also confusing to us earthlings. We may realize, unlike the alien, that normality in the TV world is rather different from normality of the world beyond it. But because we spend so much time watching television, we are prone to lose our grip on distinctions between the two. A good example is *The Cosby Show*, which is about a professional family whose social class makes it unusual in the real world but decidedly average among the privileged populace of television. So, do we see its members as normal or as belonging to a privileged class?

One of the most striking features of our audience study is the ability of most people to see it both ways at the same time: to combine an awareness of the Huxtables' upper middle class status with the idea that they are a normal, everyday family. These contesting strains of thought were manifested repeatedly. The apparent contradiction is only resolved if we make the distinction between the TV world and the world beyond it. One group of respondents saw the Huxtables as "very typical" and "universal" in one context and "kind of a highbrow, upper middle class professional family" in another. Thus we are able, as this white working class viewer did, to see the Huxtables as both typical and atypical:

The little sister is adorable. I like to see the interaction. I think it's very typical. I think it's great to show that they're just like we are, in fact, they're higher socially than we are, have more money.

The Cosby Show has a particular place within the genre of situation comedy. It has developed a style that is credible rather than ridiculous.

It explores the comic potential of the everyday, offering us neither slapstick nor absurdity. As one respondent put it: "They keep themselves down to earth" so that they appear to be, in the words of another, "just like any other family." In some ways, the show has successfully incorporated the day-to-day realism of soap opera, without the melodrama, into situation comedy. As we watch the characters develop through a myriad of everyday, domestic events, they take on a three-dimensional quality; the more stereotypical characterizations common to African-American sitcoms are avoided.

The notion that the Huxtable family is "just like a real family" was one of the most powerful themes running through our focus group discussions. Few respondents saw *The Cosby Show* as simply an enjoyable fantasy; rather, the show was praised repeatedly for its "realistic" and "believable" qualities. These qualities were grounded in the viewers' perceptions of their own reality. The Huxtables were "real," in other words, because they were "regular," "everyday," and "typical"—just like the viewer.

The plausibility of such an assessment, we might suppose, depends upon similarities between the viewers' world and the world they are watching. Middle class viewers should, for example, find it easier than working class viewers to relate to an upper middle class television family like the Huxtables. What we discovered in this connection was rather surprising: in most cases, working class respondents were just as likely to relate the Huxtables' world to their own as middle or upper middle class respondents. The reality of television, in other words, does *not* seem to rest upon the reality of the viewers' own environment.

The following comments were all made by people whom we might expect to have little in common with the Huxtables—working class white people:

> [The Cosby Show *is*] *really making a satire of life the way they're doing it, average everyday things that happen every day.* . . . *Because what they do, is they really carry it off and say these are the things that can happen to anybody, I don't care if you're white, black, pink, yellow, or green; this happens to everybody in everyday life. That's what they do. They just satirize everything that happens in normal life.*

> *It's good family humor. You can put yourself in that situation, and I can see where it can happen; and it really makes fun of the everyday type of thing and all that.*

> [Compared to other black sitcoms] *Cosby is much better.* . . . *The actors are much better, a lot funnier, more stuff you can relate to, they're a lot funnier than the other two.* . . . *Like* Amen, *the daughter*

who dates the priest, or whatever he is, you know she's just not realistic, from my point of view anyway. With 227 and Jackie, I don't relate to her or care for her at all as an actress, and she's hardly a realistic person. You can get involved in The Cosby Show *and feel that you understand it; you're a part of it and can relate to it while on these other shows there's not even usually a whole plot; it's just kind of there.*

It's an all-round easy-going atmosphere. . . . It's just family oriented, where you can relate to something it brings to mind in yourself. It's not too far-fetched; some sitcoms get so far out.

Those teasing moments they had, when she found the magazine, you know, and he was saying "Oh, I read it for the articles"; you know, that's the kind of humor I kind of relate to, you know; you grow up that way. . . . That's just so normal, it would happen like that.

[I can] relate to it a little more than the others. The others seem to be, I mean, that Amen *is not quite a family show. I don't think it's . . . although some people's families are like that. I shouldn't say that; it's just not like ours.*

It is interesting to note that the sitcoms these respondents dismiss as being less realistic (and more difficult to relate to) contain characters who are, in a material sense, much closer to themselves than the Huxtables are.

The ability of working class people to relate to the Huxtables has also been observed in a recent study of female audiences by Andrea Press (1991: 156):

Cosby is another show which garners praise from working-class women for its overall portrayal of American family life. Several working-class women, when initially describing the show, immediately bring up their belief that Cosby is a show that portrays a "typical" family. . . . "I watch the Bill Cosby show. It's an average family, working parents, nice house, not wealthy but . . . and that to me is more an American family, you know. Like people from other countries see Dallas and Dynasty, they think that's how we all live. Watch Cosby; I think that's more of a typical American family."

The Cosby Show is playing a kind of conjuring trick with its viewers, one that is made possible by the distorted image of the world that television in the United States presents. The Huxtables are an upper middle class professional family, and we can recognize them as such. Yet within the middle class world of television, the Huxtables are no longer privileged but normal, "basically a regular family." Thus working class viewers can relate to a family that, in the world beyond television, would be separated and distanced from them by the many class barriers that determine our social lives.

Press discovered that the viewers most critical of the show's lack of realism were not working class but middle class. Although this finding was also apparent in our study, middle and upper middle class respondents were still able to identify with *The Cosby Show* in much the same way. The following comments are from white middle class respondents:

> *We were in Provincetown, at a nightclub; there was one of those female impersonators. And this announcer came out and did a little comedy routine. There were a lot of same-sex couples in the audience. He took one look at Harriet and I in the front row and said, "Oh, the Cosbys are here too." He had us pegged.*

> *[Regarding Theo's sisters teasing him,] I could feel a sense of annoyance, because I have little cousins who do that! So I can relate to that.*

> *The one point where the men are trying to sneak out to play the game. . . . I was just thinking, we're having the Superbowl this Sunday, and I don't know where I'm going to be Sunday, but I can just picture the same sort of thing happening . . . or I thought of Thanksgiving where that will happen.*

> *What makes it funny is that it's humor around universal developmental issues, the kind of stuff that adolescents go through, the kind of stuff that young-marrieds go through, the kind of stuff you go through with your first baby, your first job. They're situations that everybody can relate to and in which nobody has to get put down; you don't have to be really crass. And I think that's one of the really nice things about the show.*

> *Just a typical scene of American families . . . something that probably occurs in every household.*

> *[Regarding* A Different World*] I watched it a couple of times, and I didn't care for it too much. . . . I didn't think the characters were as realistic. I think I like this because, yeah, and we have three kids too, and you could, I could, relate. I related to so much of some of the things that took place, I think that's why I like that one better.*

The very title of *The Cosby Show*, we should remember, encourages viewers to assume it has a real-life identity. The lead character, Bill Cosby, plays with the boundaries of fact and fiction by blurring the line between himself and the character he plays. Dr. Heathcliff Huxtable and Bill Cosby are, in this sense, the same person. The viewers we spoke to would often refer to the Huxtable family as "the Cosbys," a confusion facilitated by the well-known similarities between Bill Cosby's real family and his televisual one. The notion that the Huxtable family is based upon the real-life Cosby household increases its claims to verity, clinching the perception that what we are watching is, indeed, just like real life:

I kind of think Bill Cosby could be Cliff Huxtable.

I like it. I think that's the way he is really, in real life with his own kids. I'll bet that's how he is. . . . That's how he is as a father, he's not acting.

The proof of the Huxtables, in other words, is Bill Cosby himself. As one respondent put it: "I like Bill Huxtable."

COSBY CONTRADICTIONS

One distinction we can make between the responses of middle class groups and working class groups was that, despite being much closer to the Huxtables' world, middle class viewers were much more likely to add caveats to their praise for the show's realism. There appear to be two reasons for this: middle class viewers feel a greater obligation to be critical of television (as a form of intellectual display), and they are in a better position to judge what is, for a professional family, realistic. Other studies (Press, 1991; Morley, 1986) suggest that, in much the same way, working class viewers are more able to question the realism of working class TV characters.

What does the ability to question *The Cosby Show*'s realism signify? Our findings suggest that it means remarkably little beyond a tolerance for the kind of cognitive dissonance we have already described.

Many of these interviews followed the same pattern. Group members would begin by praising *The Cosby Show* for its "realistic," "true-to-life," and "everyday" representation of a "typical" family. Later in the discussion, the same respondents would criticize the show for its *failure* to be "realistic" or "believable." The coexistence of these contradictory attitudes was never resolved or (with one exception) confronted: the later judgment did not appear in any way to negate the earlier one. One respondent, for example, singled the show out as more "believable" than other situation comedies:

I would say that they appear to be a little bit more of a, like believable as real people. . . . Granted, um, they're a well-off family, and they may not be like most real people, but they're believable people as opposed to some.

When the discussion shifted toward individual characters, however, this respondent made the following observation:

> *I don't see him as a doctor. You never see him as a doctor. . . . He's not going to be home that much. . . . You never see him in his office; he's home all of the time, and he's essentially home more than his wife is. . . . He's a house husband, that's what he is. Um, so as a working man that's supposed to be a doctor and all of that,* it's just totally unbelievable.

The show's characters are, at one moment, "believable as real people" and "totally unbelievable" at another.

Another group found the show "very realistic":

> *I think the way that he [Cliff] deals with people is pleasant and realistic. I think the way he deals with the kids and stuff, in terms of being stern and yet making jokes at the same time, is also very realistic. . . . I think he's a believable character.*

—and yet "not realistic":

> *Well, we've talked about this about a lot of shows—he's never busy. He's never working, it's not realistic. . . . The time factor of the parents is usually so unrealistic. They're working, but yet they're never really frenzied, and they have so much time and energy to put into each of their kids' problems.*

These apparently contradictory judgments are possible because the viewer is speaking (albeit not self-consciously) from two different points of view. When the show is praised for its realism, the viewer feels a closeness and an intimacy with the show. As these respondents put it:

> *I think that Cosby is much more true to life [than other sitcoms]; you can put yourself right into the picture. Just about everything they do has happened to you, or you've seen it happen.*

> *There's no stereotype whatsoever, in these people [on* The Cosby Show*]. I think everybody can relate to somebody in that show—black, white, anybody.*

Yet, when the viewer imposes a sense of critical distance, the show suddenly looks very different:

> *That show shows a really unrealistic view. I mean, can you think of anyone whose wife is a lawyer, and the husband's a doctor? I'm talking anyone. I mean, that's blowing off the spectrum. And then if*

you talk about black or white children, or anybody, that are raised in this area, there's no way that they can really get the proper upbringing.

I don't think he [Cliff Huxtable] is a doctor type at all. . . . He's always happy, always rested, never on call. . . .

And never sued in five years that he's been on. An obstetrician, in five years of practice, would be sued, I'm sorry.

As these comments suggest, the show's perceived realism is a source of pleasure, enabling the viewer to identify with the characters and situations on the screen and to incorporate these identifications into their own lives. Viewers were therefore apt to link their enjoyment with their belief in the show's world: in this mood it is, as one white middle class viewer put it, "believable, and you laugh, and you relax, and it flows along." In many of the group discussions, there was a gradual shift to more critical and analytical thinking, to a perspective in which the show's status *as a TV program* is foregrounded. In the groups quoted here, the discussion moved from a comfortable and enjoyable acceptance of the show's realism toward a more critical appraisal. From this critical distance, it becomes appropriate to emphasize the *differences* between the show's world and viewers' perceptions of reality. This, ultimately, leads to the generally dismissive assertion that, after all, "it is a comedy. You can't expect it to be realistic."

It is significant, in this respect, that the one white respondent who saw *only* the fairy-tale side of the Huxtable family was also the only white viewer in our study to actively dislike the show:

If you're looking at the real world . . . [Roseanne] is much closer. And people don't like that. That's why [Cosby] is such a beautiful fairy-tale. Because it is so unreal in relationship to most people's lives.

My God, you're going to bring a crack house into Cosby? *Come on, where do you think all the crack houses are? Who in hell do you think's running the crack houses? You think these are all white people selling dope? No! It's all his people selling dope, running the crack houses, and having all the problems. But we're not going to talk about that in this show. This is the show that ignores 100 percent of all the problems that exist in this country.*

The only black group to unambiguously reject *The Cosby Show* did so for much the same reason, even if the reality they are measuring the show against is rather different:

The whole show is fake to me. It's just fake. . . . That show tonight, none of that was real. Like the two guys were out there, in the cold. What was it they were playing? . . . Hey, you don't see no black people doing that. They sit around watching football games and drinking beer. You know what I'm saying? It's just . . . it ain't real.

I can't stand her [Clair]. . . . Because she's not a typical black person. She walks around dressed up all the time, now come on. We don't walk around dressed up all the time. She's a lawyer and we understand that. She comes home from work . . . how come her hair's not in rollers? How come she can't walk around with her blue jeans on? . . . You know what I'm saying? Now come on.

[Theo]'s not your average black teenager either. Because the way he's under his mama all the time. . . . They're not like that. They say "hi," and they play their jiving music, as I call it; and no, not a black typical teenager. [He's] different from my two brothers. His room is always clean, and you never see him arguing—and my brothers argue all the time, call each other names and, you know.

These respondents' unusually vehement dismissals were based upon an inability to accept as real the images offered. Unlike most other viewers, they were simply unable to suspend disbelief.

The fact that the contradictory responses are more common suggests that our attitudes toward television are complex and ambiguous. Among other things, it reveals that the ability to construct a critical view of televisual realism does not immunize us from confusing television with reality. We may be as capable of dismissing *The Cosby Show* as "totally unbelievable" as we are of immersing ourselves in its "reality." The realization that the show is a fantasy does not stop us from discussing it as if it were not; as one white woman put it, "I forget sometimes, it's just a show, you know."

The implications of this are profound. We can no longer assume that the content of TV fiction does not matter simply because TV viewers understand that it is fiction.

THE WORLD ACCORDING TO *COSBY*

We have detailed the ways in which TV viewers assimilate *The Cosby Show* into their worldview to emphasize the significance of such assimilations. Our study suggests that *The Cosby Show* has the capacity to influence people's perceptions of the world. It is from this starting point that we shall build our argument about the role of *The Cosby Show* in contemporary U.S. culture.

However skeptical we sometimes appear, most of us place a frightening degree of faith in television images. Andrea Press (1991: 163) recounts a conversation that exemplifies this trust: the discussion turns to women attorneys, and the respondent is asked to compare the only attorney she knows with the fictional attorney, Clair Huxtable:

INTERVIEWER: *You know one woman attorney. Did she remind you of Clair?*

RESPONDENT: *No. Not even closely. Because she wasn't as feminine as Clair Huxtable.*

INTERVIEWER: *Who do you think is more typical of women attorneys?*

RESPONDENT: *Clair Huxtable.*

INTERVIEWER: *Why?*

RESPONDENT: *Well, because I've seen other ones on television like on the news and things like that and they are all more feminine than the one I knew.*

This response is, in one sense, quite remarkable: TV images are not only trusted; they are given more credence than real-life experience. The respondent does attempt to legitimate her evaluation by referring to lawyers "on the news" (i.e., *real* lawyers) rather than in drama series like *LA Law, Equal Justice,* or *The Cosby Show.* However, because women attorneys are so rare on TV news and so plentiful in TV fiction, it is probable that her judgment is based more on the latter than the former.

Once we begin to think how central television is in most people's lives, this judgment, this faith in televisual truth, becomes less remarkable and more understandable. Because fictional characters invited into our homes come to appear routine or commonplace or predictable, we are bound to become more credulous.

What makes *The Cosby Show* particularly worthy of consideration is the fact that all its leading characters are black. Although (as we shall shortly demonstrate) *The Cosby Show* is no longer exceptional in its nonstereotypical portrayal of African Americans, it has shifted the TV world toward a new vision, a world in which blacks, and, moreover, *realistic* blacks, can be members of upper middle class society.

This shift, as we shall later suggest, is of great consequence. For the time being, let us simply assert that *The Cosby Show* matters because it informs people in the United States about the position of African Americans in the society.

The respondents in our study, both black and white, had no difficulty making statements about black people based upon their experience of the Huxtables. The whites' statements often amounted to observations about black people in general, observations that their actual experience of black people did not equip them to make. The following remarks from two middle class and two working class white respondents were typical:

> It looks to me in the family, that she [Clair] . . . that she's really the driving force behind the family. . . . I think that's very common, for one thing, in many black households.

> But look how far we've come from the days of Archie Bunker, you know, when a black. . . . He was tolerant . . . but it was a different kind of tolerance; it was almost like he was being a big guy . . . to include them. . . . So now, I think it's good for people to see black families can own nice homes and have careers and have nice clothes and have goals for their children, where for so long, it was never even thought of, considered.

> I think there's a lot of black families out there that are similar to the Cosbys that they're not such a stereotype black. You know, talking like the blacks' slang or that kind of stuff . . . being portrayed as intelligent, white-collar workers and that kind of thing. I should think, from a black perspective, The Cosby Show is more complimentary to blacks than some of the other shows. You know, the 227, the older woman hanging out of the window watching the neighbors walk by and stuff like that, which is reality in a lot of situations; but in terms of . . . it just seems to be heavy into black stereotyping.

> I like the fact that they're black and they present a whole other side of what you tend to think black families are like.

It is interesting to note that these remarks include the phrase "I think" or "you tend to think," thereby acknowledging, albeit implicitly, that their understanding of what the show tells them about black people is not always confirmed by their own experience.

White viewers were a little more confident when they used the show to determine differences between black and white behavior; this respondent, for example, could speak from a position of at least partial knowledge:

> Their [the Huxtables'] antics are just so . . . I mean white people don't act like that . . . just even their expressions.

> A white person or someone else would be more tense. . . . I would tend to say most white people, if we're going to generalize, then I'd say white people, are much more tight, uptight. Like I can just see a white mother coming in and flipping out.

Although this respondent can assume knowledge of white people, both statements contain an assumption that was rarely challenged in the white focus groups, namely, television and *The Cosby Show* tell us something about black people. In the next chapter we will examine the nature of people's attraction to the Huxtables and how the strength of that attraction places *The Cosby Show* in a privileged position with respect to the ways in which U.S. society understands race relations.

3

The Success of *Cosby*

*I*n the previous chapter we argued that television affects how viewers make sense of the world. It is not usually one episode or one series that influences the way we think; it is the aggregate of messages that enter our minds. These messages are part of our environment and, now that television has become ubiquitous, are consumed as automatically and unconsciously as the air we breathe.

Why, then, have we chosen to focus on a particular series in our analysis of contemporary television? And why *The Cosby Show*? *The Cosby Show* deserves this attention not simply because of its tremendous and enduring popularity but because it has influenced the way black people are represented on prime-time television generally. As we will demonstrate in the next chapter, the ratings success of the series has unleashed a host of black upper middle class characters across prime-time television. The show's impact upon the content of prime time goes far beyond the cozy Huxtable home. The show has been pivotal in redefining the way African Americans are depicted on television in the 1990s.

In this chapter, we consider what lies behind the power and influence of *The Cosby Show*. Few persons, inside or outside network television, would have predicted that the show would have such an impact. Why has *The Cosby Show* been so successful?

To answer this question fully, we need to address at least three different but connected issues. First, what is there in the show's writing and acting that attracts viewers? How, in other words, does the content of the show relate to people's needs and desires? Second, what is omitted from the show that, if present, would change viewers' identification and support? What does it not talk about; what themes cannot be introduced (without endangering the level of viewer support)? Third, what are the broader social and cultural contexts that make the show's content resonate with meaning and significance? What are the currents within the broader

35

society that make *The Cosby Show* so important for viewers? In this chapter we will deal mainly with the first of these issues, leaving the others for later chapters.

At one level, *The Cosby Show* is involved quite explicitly with issues of representation. In a society that is still largely divided along racial lines, the series is concerned with presenting images of a black family that are both positive and popular. In so doing, it addresses its white and black audiences in different ways.

For the white audience, it wants to make racial differences irrelevant. The white audience must be able to look at the Huxtables not simply as a black family but as an "Everyfamily." White viewers must be able to appreciate, understand, and identify with the Huxtables without forgetting that they are actually looking at a black family. It asks white viewers to accept a black family as "one of them," united by commonalities rather than divided by race. If *The Cosby Show* succeeds in this laudable mission (and we shall demonstrate that in many ways it does), then it would be easy to argue that the series plays a positive and progressive role within a racially divided society.

For the black audience, the series wants to provide a mirror that does not reflect the prejudices and stereotypes of white perception but instead shows black people as they would like to recognize themselves—strong, independent, intelligent—a mirror that shows the *dignity* of black American life. There is evidence from our interviews that black viewers evaluate the show in precisely this way.

The remainder of this chapter examines these issues in relation to white and black viewers more closely. Although the tone of this chapter is celebratory, we warn the reader that this celebration is only short-lived. The show's influence goes beyond its noble intentions. Later in this book, we shall demonstrate that the show has less salutary ideological repercussions, which clearly were not envisaged by its makers.

WHITE VIEWERS AND POPULARITY: THE SAME AND DIFFERENT

It became obvious during our interviews that Bill Cosby's presence as a comedian is an important part of the show's popularity. We have already suggested that Bill Cosby, the actor, and Cliff Huxtable, the character, often merge into a single identity: For many, Bill Cosby *is* Cliff Huxtable. The Cosby-Huxtable persona was specifically identified, by almost all of our white interviewees, as a significant part of the show's appeal. The following comments from a variety of white respondents are typical:

The way he acts, it's really good . . . his expressions and all that stuff. I don't think anyone could really get that across, like he does.

I think that he's very funny. I don't think it would be as funny—he's very funny. He has a lot to do with it, all of it together.

You have to remember that black or white, Bill Cosby is such an amazing talent that I mean, if he were Hispanic and had an Hispanic family, it would still be the top.

It's his facial actions; it's his body language.

He's so likable, and I get the feeling if he were your neighbor or your relative, you'd love to see him come in. I do, anyway. I think he's just a real nice guy.

The one white respondent who disliked the show (dismissing it for its sugar candy fluffiness) was still enthusiastic about the actor behind Cliff Huxtable: "I just love the man." When this viewer watched, he watched for Cosby and not the show. For this viewer, Bill Cosby transcended race—he was neither black nor white. Cosby "is a special person. You can't really put him in a context with all of television, because he is exceptional." This "transcendental" quality was frequently alluded to, as this upper middle class man put it:

When we see Bill Cosby in concert, I don't look at a black person. I see Bill Cosby up there. . . . If he was white, I think I would still enjoy his humor as much.

As indispensable as Bill Cosby is to the success of the series, it is more than simply a showcase for his comic talent. He is backed up by creative writers and a cast able to carry through his vision in a way that creates a powerful bond with a diverse audience. Apart from specific references to Bill Cosby the comedian, four additional popular themes emerged from our interviews with white respondents.

The first, oft-repeated theme was the show's ability to present everyday events and activities believably and realistically. The second theme appears to contradict the first: namely, the pleasure brought about by the show's elements of fantasy. We found that viewers seemed to enjoy the show's realism and escapism at the same time. Third, a number of viewers enjoyed the show's depictions of the minutiae of family life. Finally, the Huxtables appear to reflect a black culture that white audiences enjoy being exposed to (in many cases because of its familiarity rather than its difference). It is the intermingling of these themes that allows the show's style and content to interact so positively with the needs and attitudes of the white audience.

"THEY'RE THINGS THAT HAPPEN DAY BY DAY"

Most white respondents' initial answers to the question "What do you like about the show?" centered, curiously enough, on its apparent ordinariness, on its ability to capture the typical, mundane aspects of everyday life and to draw humor from them. As a female respondent put it in comparing the show to other sitcoms:

> I think that Cosby is much more true to life; you can put yourself right into the picture. Just about everything they do has happened to you, or you've seen it happen.

The fact that the show breaks from the normal narrative mold of television drama, in which the bizarre and the dramatic become the norm, was regarded with relief and pleasure by many white viewers:

> So The Cosby Show, what we've seen of it, there aren't many crises; they're things that happen day by day.

> In real families you don't have an outrageous situation every week.

> It is more realistic than most of the other sitcom shows. . . . This could happen. I could see this type of thing happening. . . . The other shows I think you have to suspend [dis]belief.

In relation to the particular episode that respondents watched before the interviews, many male viewers identified strongly with the competition between Cliff and Dr. Harman. Clearly, competition and fraternity accord with many men's perceptions of their masculinity. The show, in characteristic style, succeeds in poking fun at this aspect of "masculinity" without actually undermining it, as these comments suggest:

> I liked when they were arguing about which ball was closest, because I can imagine competitions I've had with my friends or relatives who are close; it's almost juvenile that you're doing it, but it's the nature of the sport nonetheless. That really conjured up images in myself.

> I could relate to Cliff and his doctor friend wanting to sneak away from the girls and wanting to go out and play a sport 'cause they were both looking forward to it all week and had balls in hand when they met; and Clair was determined to have them stay in and enjoy conversation with the men. . . . I could associate with that as a sports addict myself. Wanting to go outside while the girls enjoy themselves and their own company while the girls wanted me to stick around and have a good time with them.

> *I guess sometimes when me and my buddies are playing games and things, we get into the same kind of thing, about quarreling about the ball or how close it was, or something; even when we're playing badminton, we'll argue about who got the point and who didn't.*

The identification between the viewers and the events depicted in the series runs so deep that the Huxtables are frequently seen as behavioral models. Cosby, like a televisual version of Abigail Van Buren or Ann Landers, advises us on how to live our own lives. One female respondent, for example, confessed to being "not mature" enough in handling her own problems with male teenage sons and sex magazines after she saw the way that Clair handled such a problem. She wished that she had handled a similar situation as Clair had:

> *I had to laugh because the only time that I found girly magazines in my son's room, first of all they knew it was something I wouldn't approve of, was when I turned the mattress one time. . . . There were like three copies of one of those magazines, which I definitely would not have wanted in the house, and I remember taking them downstairs and burning them in the incinerator. I did not behave maturely and say, you know . . . it was after I burned them that I said, you know, "This morning when I was turning your mattress I discovered something under the, you know, that really kind of bothered me and if you're looking for them, they're gone." Now that wasn't very mature, but that was my reaction; I mean, it was totally different than hers.*

These comments suggest that the series does more than pleasantly wash over its viewers; it touches them, creating feelings of involvement and intimacy. This level of identification is important because it suggests that the series has a more profound influence than a show that is passively consumed and subsequently forgotten.

Although viewers referred generally to the typicality of the Huxtable family, Theo, their only son (played by Malcolm Jamal Warner), seems to be a key figure in the construction of this "ordinary family." Respondents often referred to him as a "typical teenager" and usually as someone they liked. As one of our female respondents put it: "He is an awfully nice kid. I mean, if you could have a teenage boy who was like him, you'd be so lucky." Despite this comment, this likability is not based upon perfection—quite the contrary. It is his amiable awkwardness and foolishness that make him so "typical" and so likable:

> *He's a typical juvenile boy . . . any teenage boy that sees a girl that he says he's attracted to is going to fall and do stupid things like he did and make a fool of himself in front of her.*

I compare myself to him, when I was in high school; and he's not a show-off or nothing, he's just someone in the family.

Theo is more your typical boy, you know, scatterbrained. He gets himself in trouble; he doesn't do as well in school. We find out this year that he was dyslexic.

In the episode that had just been viewed, Theo is trying very hard to impress a young lady (Lindy) who is visiting the Huxtables with her parents. His clumsy teenage machismo is seen as endearingly ordinary by women:

That's very realistic. . . . That's what boys are like. . . . They'll make up things like they're interested.

and, in a rather different way, by men:

I can kind of sympathize with . . . Theo, in the awkward position; here's this gorgeous smart girl who's doing a lot of neat things, and he starts feeling kind of weird about it. I get brought back to that sense of being nervous. This new person you don't know, you're not fully in touch with what's making you feel funny around this person; but you can watch him stumble all over himself—I can pretty much relate to that.

One notable thing about these viewers' comments is not only what is said but the *way* it is said. Theo is discussed as a real person. One female respondent, for example, made the following comment about Theo's personality:

I think he's the only son in the family and that perhaps, I think, maybe makes him more social.

This is a thoughtful psychoanalytic comment about a character who, lest we forget, does not actually exist. One male viewer similarly analyzed the relationship between Theo and his father with approval:

I don't like his character on certain levels, but I like the relationship between his father and him. It looks to me like . . . that Cliff really has Theo as his favorite. He got all these girls, but he's only got this one son. One son to carve the turkey, one son to do this, etc.

Other viewers talked about the delight they experienced at seeing Theo's interactions with his buddy Cockroach:

> *But the two of them together is a riot. I mean, they work and talk so easily together over mutual problems, and it's really a delight to watch.*

Perhaps the best assessment was given by a male respondent who observed of Theo:

> *That's real real because he's got the picture-perfect parents and he's a D–C student. So that's real. That's* real *real!*

"IT HAS THAT KIND OF AIRBRUSHED QUALITY ABOUT IT"

As we observed in the previous chapter, in the course of the interview viewers would move from talking about the typicality of the Huxtables to commenting on their fairy-tale lives without any apparent sense of contradiction. Many comments revolved around Clair Huxtable. Few white respondents referred to her, in contrast to Theo, as typical. Clair is, in fact, admired for being atypical and a positive role model. The following comments reflect the degree of respect that she commands from the audience:

> *I like what she does with her children as far as she can "swipe and dype" them; she's almost like a cat, you know. She can "swipe and dype" them in loving care and kindness to them, you know . . . like a lioness, you know. You sit there and see a lioness that is very proud and protects her cubs and everything.*

> *It's a perfect image of a working mother. She stands for what she thinks and all that stuff. Doesn't take any back talk.*

> *She's a very good representation of women. I think she carries off the whole scene . . . with humor and dignity and intelligence. And confidence. . . . She dresses beautifully, yeah. And she always looks so beautifully groomed. Yeah, she's an inspiration.*

> *She's gorgeous, she's well educated, she's well dressed, has a good sense of humor. She deals with the kids, certainly not like in real life, 'cause she's never angry, never loses her cool, but she's fun to watch.*

Notice the connection in this last comment: "certainly not like in real life . . . but she's fun to watch." This sense of the show as fantasy, escape, and entertainment seems to contradict the celebration of the ordinary. How can we resolve this paradox? Many viewers referred to the show as being "easy" to watch and resisted any suggestions that might have dragged the Huxtables down into "harder" territory (for instance, questions about what the show would look like if the Huxtables were working class). This suggests that when people praise the show for its realism, this is not a straightforward reference to some objective state of affairs. It is, rather, an easy realism that people desire and not the sort that reminds them of the unpleasantness of ordinary life. The following comments reflect this attraction to an easy believability:

> It's things that could happen and situations that are very close to children growing up. . . . They always look nice too; . . . they have ethics. They're neat and they always look nice.

> Right; believable and you laugh and you relax, kind of and it flows along, but the other thing [other sitcoms] . . . the yelling and the screaming, I just, I don't know.

The Cosby Show appears to have cultivated a space where fantasy and reality are allowed to merge—without our suffering any philosophical qualms. As a male respondent put it: "It has that kind of airbrushed quality about it—everybody's a little too cute in the things they do, but aside from that, it still seems more realistic." This response was, nevertheless, unusual in its direct juxtaposition of the two responses. Most viewers tended to talk about fantasy and reality at different and discrete moments. The following comment is by a female respondent who had earlier praised the show for its realism:

> But maybe what you love about them too is that nobody wants to see repeats of what they're living. . . . It's totally a fantasy to me, a fairy tale; where I think if you bring in the real humdrum of what really life is all about, it would be a total bore, tragic smashing bore. The everyday struggle of living, I don't think people really want to see that all the time; they live it too much, they don't want to see that. They say "Please give me somethin' extra funny and special," and "Oh, look at their gorgeous sweaters." I would much prefer to see a little bit of fairy tale and make-believe rather than reality one-on-one because we know reality, we live it daily. . . . It [The Cosby Show] is entertainment.

The references to the sweaters and the immaculately designed backgrounds were very strong in the white responses, particularly in working or lower middle class focus groups. Upper middle class respondents, however, were more likely to use the notion of fantasy pejoratively. For working class respondents, the enjoyment was more self-consciously aesthetic:

This is nice, it looks good and it's kind of, you accept it; they have a beautiful home and everything is okay.

I liked the background. I like to look at the background on a TV program, I enjoy that. I don't enjoy dismal backgrounds. . . . The setting, the clothes, that type of thing. And I enjoy watching Phylicia Rashad.

Here we need to pay attention to what is *left out* of the picture that makes it more attractive to white viewers (we will examine this issue more closely in a later chapter). The celebration of what is essentially an upper middle class lifestyle is the flip side of the rejection of a working class lifestyle. Indeed, it is this rejection of the discussion of broader societal issues in favor of interpersonal and family relations that appears to be the key to the popularity of the show:

I like the fact that they're not a working family. The money just seems to be there; they don't even seem to be working. A working class family, you'd almost draw relations to, they'd have troubles at work, or something like that, so you'd start thinking about something you'd have to do at work. It's almost a separation from that. It's never real issues in the real world; it's always family matters.

"IT'S ALWAYS FAMILY MATTERS"

Although identification with individuals and with specific situations is an important factor in the show's appeal, we found that it was the Huxtable *family* that attracted many people. The show's emphasis on family dynamics was a constant topic of focus group discussions, particularly for women. The following comments were made by women from a variety of class backgrounds:

They're always very warm. . . . They have a real, real family.

Family issues. . . . The real true family things. . . . I think it's more of a typical family.

Basically a regular family.

I like the sense of family they portray. The family is a real tight unit. The mother and father get along, and they give a sense of that to their children, I think, so that the family is real important to them and they solve their conflicts in their family.

It's also extended family, yeah; it's his parents, her parents, the grandparents are a type or part of the family. . . . It's like everything is pulled into the family instead of the family just separating and all doing their own thing.

The broader sociocultural reasons for such strong identification are beyond the scope of our study, although we did find hints in our respondents' comments about the emotional needs that the show might be addressing. One woman in her early twenties speculated that the stress on family themes and situations resonates particularly strongly with people who have seen their own families disintegrate:

> *The show is successful because it's a family unit, and nowadays, that's real hard. . . . A lot [more] of my friends have parents that are divorced than parents that are still together. . . . I know with my friends, that everyone is looking for that stability.*

The same woman also claimed that *The Cosby Show* played an important ritualistic function in the mid-1980s in university dormitories:

> *. . . six girls, so it was like, all of us would go and it was either, one person's room, we'd go in to somebody's room and we'd like pack in the room and sit down and watch this snowy TV, but we had to watch Cosby.*

The stressing of family themes is nevertheless not enough to generate the type of emotional bonding that we discovered in our interviews (after all, literally hundreds of series have attempted to use this strategy of identification). To understand this requires filling out the "content" of the family themes. Cliff Huxtable's character seems to be key to this. A number of people mentioned how much they liked the way he interacted within the family:

> *I like how he plays it with children; I like his role with them. Because he treats them not as equals, but he doesn't look down on them and treat them like he's the father or the image of anything.*

> *I basically love watching him [Bill Cosby], in that father role when all the kids are going crazy. It reminds me, well, my family's obviously a lot different. But it kind of reminds me of what it must have been like for our parents who had tons of kids around. Those moments when you're like, "oh man, too many kids."*

Parents in particular responded positively to the models of family discipline the show provides:

> *I get a kick out of the way that the Cosbys discipline their children. . . . It's always done with humor.*

> *One thing I like about the show is that the parents are always seen as the ultimate authority and that their role is not questioned. . . . The kids still see the parents as the ultimate authority within the family structure, which the majority of shows today don't do any longer.*

The result of such bonding and identification is to grant the Huxtables a privileged place in viewers' lives in terms of how viewers saw themselves. Many viewers remarked that the Huxtables reminded them of their own families so that watching the show is like holding up a mirror to a pleasant time gone by. We are watching our own past with more than a hint of nostalgia.

> *He's what I think a father should be; and a mother. . . . They both are there for their kids. That's what it portrays to me. . . . I don't think of them as black. . . . They're just people and they are nice and they treat their children good and they seem to get through all the situations pretty well; and I like the wisecracks, which reminds me of my own very much.*

> *I enjoy it just as much [now as before] because my kids grew at the same time so I could relate to a lot of the things going on as the kids got older.*

This was a recurring theme: the Huxtables were like friends whom we had seen grow up and go through different stages. The audience and the family had taken the same journey:

> *[The show] has progressed the way the family progresses anyway.*

> *I've been watching it for years and I know all the kids' names and everything. I've been watching it for so long. I've watched them go from small to where they are in college now.*

The strength of the familial reflections is so strong that, although viewers were aware that family relationships were idealized representations, even white viewers identified with the Huxtables:

> *My sister once said that our family reminded her of the Cosby family . . . because my husband, he acts a little bit like Cosby a lot.*

> *You can just identify with this family, even if they're a different race.*

"*THE COSBY SHOW*'S BLACK, AND THAT FITS"

Does this form of close identification between white viewers and the Huxtables mean that race has ceased to be a factor in the appeal of the show? Are the Huxtables, for white viewers, so like "us" that they are seen as white? On one level, this is undoubtedly so. We should be careful, however, not to misinterpret this response. For white respondents to see the Huxtables as "just like white people" (as most of them did) requires *first* distinguishing them as black *before* assimilating them into their own (white) cultural milieu. Consequently, in what appears to be an embrace of a liberal, nonracist consciousness, the fact that the Huxtables are black is seen by many as a good thing. These are some of the most enthusiastic comments on this point:

> But it makes it more interesting to me because he's black and it's so good, it adds to the show.

> It wouldn't be as fun [if the Huxtables were white]. . . . They wouldn't be into those kind of things, like when they bought this picture at one time. . . . They wouldn't get into that type of thing so much.

> It's like a little bit of America, black American history.

> I feel they bring in a lot of black culture to the show.

> I love it that it's black. And I love it because it's black because it shows a fun side of that.

> We are so wonderfully different and that's so beautifully different . . . their cultures are different, they're fabulous. No one wants to be the same as everybody else, you know.

> I'd say I'm pretty aware of it [black culture]. It seems like they're always digging into black culture somewhere along the lines of the show . . . the music. . . . They all seem to know the old jazz community. Once, one of the kids was doing a project for school, I think it was on the marches, the Civil Rights marches, and so, I think it was Theo, anyway, over the course of the show, all the grandparents came over for dinner and they all talked about what it was like to be there. . . . It seems like every show, or a lot of shows, they touch on some aspect of black heritage, so you're a little aware of it.

> The other side of the coin is they're willing to try to remind you— and I think that's fine—that this is a black family. . . . Through the

speech patterns, through the guests, through enjoyment of black culture. They've talked about black culture.

Although a majority of white viewers in our study tended to be less effusive, it was clear that the Huxtables' race, for many white viewers, was a positive thing. Certainly, these viewers were aware that they were watching a black family, but they seemed to be grateful that this was not something the show repeatedly stressed. The reminders, as befits the rest of the show's style, were gentle. One viewer contrasted *The Cosby Show* with other black sitcoms that she felt discriminated against whites. In other sitcoms, she suggested:

> *Well, they [whites] are not even hardly included in the show . . . so it's like the black community staying among itself rather than showing an integrated, you know, like you see certain shows on* Cosby *where they go to a literary meeting or something and there's a mix of whites and blacks, it's nice, seemingly, effortlessly, so it tends to remove that while keeping a black culture they obviously have.*

It is an effortless blackness. A "nice" blackness. Unlike the not-so-nice kinds of blackness exhibited on other shows:

> *I mean it's not like a jive show, like* Good Times. *I don't think it's aimed at, I think those other shows are more jive, more soul shows, say as far as the way the characters are with making you aware that they are more separate from. . . . Where* Cosby *is more of American down the line thing, which makes everybody feel accepted and being a part of watching it.*

It is important to note that this notion of "being American" does not make the Huxtables white—it extends the notion of American to include black families like the Huxtables. As a female respondent put it:

> *It fits them—like the* Golden Girls, *they're white and that fits— Cosby's show's black and that fits.*

Through this complex mixture of what is talked about and what is not, the writers and actors behind *The Cosby Show* have accomplished an exceedingly difficult task: they have made the difference of race a matter of harmony rather than division, even if only for half an hour a week.

> *It wouldn't be different if they were white, which is good because you're able to relate to them as people regardless of their color. Which I think he succeeds on in great measure that way, and eventually that's*

what we want to be able to do with all people. Just think of them as people, not as Asians, not as blacks, not as whites.

That's what the show brings across to me, that black people are just like us . . . having a regular family, the same problems just like us, having to go to work, even if you might not want to every once in a while, you know, so that's how, maybe one way they bring across that blacks are, have the same problems, likes, dislikes, that we might or might not have.

It's not an issue for me, watching the show, black or white; it all is the same in that show anyway. . . . They're just like any other family.

Many other white viewers described to us how they sometimes "forgot" that the Huxtables were black. We do not think that this is some disingenuous attempt by the respondents to appear tolerant and pluralistic. Racial difference, on *The Cosby Show,* really did not seem important to them. That white Americans living in a society still significantly divided along racial lines can view an explicitly black family as "just people" who have the same problems, dreams, and aspirations as themselves is a significant and progressive development in our popular culture. We shall deal with some of the negative aspects of this phenomenon in Chapter 6.

BLACK VIEWERS AND POPULARITY: "THANK YOU, DR. COSBY, FOR GIVING US BACK OURSELVES"

Although there are many similarities between the responses of black and white audiences (the celebration of the everydayness, the desire for family), one discourse clearly distinguishes them. The vast majority of black respondents discussed the show in a context almost entirely absent from white interviewees' comments: among black viewers, there was widespread concern about TV racial stereotyping. We will examine this in greater depth in Chapter 7, but we wish to stress that the issue of the popularity of *The Cosby Show* for black audiences has to be continually set against this backdrop. For black respondents, this was a TV program that, after years of stereotyping, showed black people as they really were. After decades in which the images of black life had been distorted by white writers and directors, *The Cosby Show* reflected a world that black Americans recognized as their own. Interviewees would no doubt endorse jazz singer Lena Horne's gratitude when she thanked Bill Cosby "for giving us back ourselves."

We will not quote black respondents at length on the themes that white audiences identified with, but we do wish to briefly demonstrate that those themes existed in the responses of the black audience. Like white respondents, black viewers found it difficult to distinguish between Bill Cosby and Cliff Huxtable, although this point revolved less around a discussion of his comic abilities and more on him as someone viewers knew well. Comparing Bill Cosby's wife to the fictional Clair Huxtable, this middle class respondent commented:

> It seems that this series really reflects his life where in real life Camille, as he said, is the backbone. And I think I kind of see that in there with Clair, and he kind of comes in there. I think he's the softer touch. I think the kids can con him a lot quicker that they can ever con Clair.

The boundary between Bill Cosby and Cliff Huxtable seems even more blurred for black audiences than for white audiences. As a black male respondent put it:

> He portrays a good father, yeah, and he portrays a good father not only on this program but it follows him off the set and on the set. . . . He always has time for the children. If they got a problem, he's always there.

Blacks also shared with whites the focus on everyday activities and concern for the family as being important in their enjoyment of the show:

> The Cosby Show *does not necessarily resolve itself. It's like daily life or life that day or whatever. It doesn't have to end and have this big triumph or whatever at the ending. It just, you know, when you go to bed at night, whatever happens that day is over and you go on to the next day, but not with some big climax at the end of each night; and that's the same way* The Cosby Show *is.*

> The family gets up, they go to school, they go to work, they come in, they have dinner together and they have the good times together, they have the bad times together, you know; and the father doesn't take any exception, you know; he treats the children they way they are supposed to be, you know? Cosby is always portraying that. . . . It's just like sitting with a family being with me when I watch the show.

This stress on the family does nevertheless appear to mean something quite specific to black viewers. The context within which black audiences locate family themes gives those themes a special significance. Specifically, this context is the discussion around the disintegration of black family life in the United States (see Chapter 4). Although white viewers (with no particular stake in the debates about the black family) saw the Huxtables as a black *family,* black viewers (with a vital stake in those debates) saw a *black* family. In contrast to the prevalent image, and indeed reality, of black families without fathers, *The Cosby Show* affirms that there is another side to the picture. A female working class respondent identified this as the context within which she found the show a source of pleasure:

> *It's a real objective story line, you know, how a black family lives and how they see things. I think that way they are trying to describe that black families are just as normal as white families. They have a functioning house, normal, just like white families.*

"WHEN I LOOK AT THEM, I LOOK AT US"

One of our main goals is to demonstrate how people derive meaning from television, not just in terms of a single program but also in terms of how the messages of television interact with discourses in other contexts. The meaning of a show is different for different audiences. Our ability to understand the significance of what audience members say depends on how well we can identify the ways in which disparate discourses interact with each other.

The level of identification of black viewers with the Huxtables is very high, and although identification occurs similarly in the white responses, its intensity for black viewers puts it on a different plane. For black respondents, the show mirrored images with which they could deeply identify. Unlike white respondents, black respondents saw themselves as personally implicated in the images they were talking about. Respondents repeatedly made statements about how they saw themselves, their fathers and mothers, their brothers and sisters, and situations from their own history in the show.

Furthermore, these statements were made with an understanding that this had not happened before on television. The pleasure of black respondents and their level of emotional bonding with the Huxtables reveal not just the creative ability of the show's writers but also the frustration that black Americans had felt with past portrayals of blacks. As a female respondent put it: "I know some of the prior black programs *I haven't found myself in.* Now like *The Jeffersons,* there's not a scene there that I can identify with."

The groups that we might expect to have identified most closely with the Huxtable family are upper middle class blacks, who really were like the Huxtables, and so they did. As this daughter of an upper middle class black family put it:

> *They dress nice. They have nice clothes. And when I look at them I look at us. Because we're not poor. We don't live in a bad community in a ghetto somewhere. We live in a nice neighborhood like they do. I go to a nice school. We have nice things. So I look at them I say that is a black family because it's like us. . . . But the three of us, we have a nice family. We, it's not like we agree all the time. Or fighting. We don't do that. So in a way we are like them.*

The strength of identification did not necessarily depend upon a viewer's class position. The sense of new discovery, of finally finding a world that they recognized (moreover a world that was a considerable source of pride and pleasure) was a constant feature of the black interviewees' responses.

> *I like Clair. I do see a lot of me in her in terms of the position that she plays and some of the situations that happen in terms of the children. . . . It's just some of the things . . . just like . . . like they saw me someplace and wrote the script, you know, and then put it on television.*

> *I love this because this is more me. And I relate to it better and I think it's. . . . It also lets my kids and my grandkids know, hey, this is what it can be if you want to. I think it will always be that way with me.*

> *That's what I was, the way she [Clair] gave the message to her son, that's the way that I always did with Brian and my children and grandchildren. You know, it's always the right message.*

> *I like a lot of things in her that remind me of myself. The one that . . . when she . . . the kid decided she didn't want to go to college. And she said, "I want my seventy thousand two hundred forty-nine dollars and two cents. And I want it now." I've felt all the money I paid for my son I'd say it comes to about that. . . . I like a lot of things she does. I like him too. He's a likable guy. I see a lot of my husband in him too.*

Black viewers continually referred to the characters of Cliff and Clair as being exactly like their parents. There is such a sense of familiarity that one female respondent felt she did not have to think when watching the show, that everything was so real that it was like living in it:

I can see some of my father in him because he's got this restraint. It says, "I'm not going to get angry." . . . Those types of things, those are real situations I can hear my parents, I can hear my father, I can hear people that I've grown up with, doing the same thing. Or thinking the same things, maybe not saying it. . . . There's something when it's extremely real, you know, some of the stuff is actually in real life versus imitating it. . . . I don't like to think when I watch that show, and I really don't have to think. It's really all right there.

The same respondent also talked about her feelings toward Clair revealing that this "hearing" of people is not some idealized representation of the past nor a longing for a golden time gone by:

I don't like to talk about Clair. I have mixed feelings about Clair. There's a tone in her voice. . . . It's an air about her sometimes that just gets in my way and I don't know what it is. . . . It's an attitude. . . . There are times when she gets that pitch in her voice that just drives me crazy. It really does because my mother had that same way. . . . I hear it in Clair and it irritates me because it used to irritate me with my mother. It's real, I guess, because people are like that, but it irritates me.

Many other viewers also talked about seeing and hearing their parents in the characters of Cliff and Clair.

My daddy can do stuff like that. He's not a joking person, but he can certainly let you know where you are, like Cliff. . . . My dad. He's like that, he's not a doctor or anything like that but the same kind of thing. . . . He's always right there in the middle whatever goes on in the family.

When Vanessa stayed out too late with her boyfriend and her mother goes—Vanessa was yelling downstairs to her boyfriend—her mother goes, "Now the next time I tell you to be quiet, I want you to do it." She was stomping up the stairs. Reminded me just of Mommy. She was stomping up those stairs. She said, "Now when I tell you to do something, you do it. You understand me?" I swear that was my mother.

But you kids have gone through that. I mean what did you say that . . . I'll always remember that first show when Bill Cosby . . . you kids kept saying, "Daddy, you write his lines?" You know your father is quick to tell you, "I brought you into this world. I will take you out."

Notice that in this next comment, a daughter in a family group who is speaking of the connection between the show and her family makes them virtually interchangeable:

> *They [Cliff and Clair] remind me of these two [parents]. Like on* The Cosby Show *when they get mad with each other over simple stuff and he tries to coax her back in. They remind me of these two. They're a trip these two.*

One respondent even talked of how she "knew" Cliff, as if she was discussing a good friend:

> *I think he's very . . . a lot like things I've seen in my husband too. And that was before I* knew *Cliff Huxtable. And it just . . . it makes him laugh at it sometimes because sometimes my kids will say, "Come here, Mom. This is you," or "That's Dad, that's Dad."*

The same types of comments were made about brothers and sisters and about specific situations the show depicted. This deep identification reinforces the link between viewers and the Huxtables. As one female respondent put it: "We're like the Cosby family."

"WHAT KIND OF QUESTION IS THAT FOR BLACK FOLK?"

It should be clear that the often told joke of *The Cosby Show* being like an Oreo cookie (black on the outside, white in the middle) would not be appreciated by our black respondents. Although there were some interesting tensions (which we examine later) regarding the Huxtables' "racial status," they were always resolved by respondents in favor of black. Overwhelmingly, the Huxtables were seen by black viewers as "really black." Although this was also the case for white respondents, they arrived at this judgment in a different way. No white viewers thought it strange to be asked how aware they were that the Huxtables are black. In contrast, though many black viewers silently granted the legitimacy of the question, some could not even comprehend it. This reaction came from an upper middle class female respondent:

> *How aware? How aware? . . . Just look at them and you can see that they are black. You're not talking to white folks now. What kind of question is that for black folk?*

When asked what made the show "black," white respondents pointed to things such as the artwork on the wall, the music in the house, and the political issues that the show raised. (The famous episode involving the march on Washington was often mentioned.) Even Hispanic respondents based their answers to this question on things such as the lack of white actors on the show, the music, the art, the politics. In short the Huxtables are black for whites and Hispanics because of the visible manifestations of black culture. They are what an outsider would see as indicators of a different culture.

Although black respondents also mentioned these visible signs of race as important, for them the most important indicators were those that an insider to the culture would recognize as defining that group: the language, the mannerisms, the "tone" and "feeling" of black life. The late English cultural theorist Raymond Williams (1961: 48) identified something that he called a "structure of feeling" that exists in every culture, the recognition of which is based upon experiencing it rather than learning about it secondhand. The responses of black audience members suggest that *The Cosby Show* has been able to capture this structure of feeling.

Often black respondents would contrast *The Cosby Show* with a white show to demonstrate its blackness:

> *I think those [white sitcoms] are unreal situations, and if the Huxtables were white, they would have to be along those lines of the* Family Ties *type thing versus the Huxtables. . . . The mannerisms and the conversations and the phrases that Bill uses are something that I think are more typical in the black family.*

> *If you take the two shows [Cosby and* Family Ties*] and, you know, put 'em side by side and give them the same scripts, I don't think they could come across as what happens in the black script and then the same thing would be the same in the white script. . . . There's just something about the way blacks do things, say things, react to things that whites would do in a different way. . . . Or sometimes it's the relationship between the father and the son. And sometimes they hit hands. And I know that whites do that now, but it seems to flow so easy when the blacks do it than when you see two white folk doing it.*

The centrality of language, not simply what is said but the way in which it is said, also emerged as a defining feature of the show's "blackness":

> *If it was a white family, I don't think I would look at it as closely, you know. It's just, you know, sometimes you can hear like Clair with a little accent to her voice; you know, like an accent that only black people would understand, you know. Just like there's slang that white people understand, there's slang that black people understand. I think that sometimes when they use that kind of language in the show*

> . . . *I mean it's not slang but just like when they have the, you know, how they dance to the jazz and everything.*

> *They do inject some things that is typical of us. They haven't lost their identity. . . . They will inject some remark or phrase that only we use.*

> *One reason is that we talk differently. I can close my eyes and tell it is a black show. They still use in the show street language, they are comfortable at home. . . . Clair is a lawyer, you never see her use legal jargon, or whatever; she talks just like a black woman. I was raised by a black man and woman and this is how they talked, so when I close my eyes I can totally tell the difference. Also we have a tone to our language and it comes from our history. It is a singing type, very melodic type of talk, or conversation that is just natural for our people. So if you are watching an all-white show, you will not hear that; you would hear the standard English. You will not hear the melodic sound of the voice as you can when the Huxtables speak.*

At other moments the comments focused on behaviors and relationships that black respondents recognized as unique to black culture:

> *I also think it said something to us about relationships between black males. See, white folks don't think that black males love each other. They don't think we love each other. They don't know that there are guys who hug and kiss as black males say "Hey man, how you doing."* . . . *I mean guys who are like family to you. Yeah, white folks need to see that.*

> *I accept them as black. . . . There are times when they do certain expressions, certain behaviors that . . . that cause you at a conscious level to acknowledge that they are a black family. . . . Most time when I'm watching, I'm just watching. . . . I know it's a black people's situation or family situation but I don't think of it.*

A number of respondents also mentioned the manner of discipline that the Huxtable parents adopt as characteristically black:

> *I just know it's a black family, that's all. . . . For instance when she's chastising a child, you very seldom see a white person chastising a child like that. . . . But I mean blacks have been chastising their children like that ever since. . . .*

It is, in sum, the "whole environment" of the Huxtable household that makes it black:

I look around and I look at the art work in their house, I listen to the slang, the black English that is used in the show, which is extremely important. I mean those are things that I happen to look at; it's the whole environment of the show which makes it black.

LOOKING ON THE BRIGHT SIDE

Thus far, it appears that *The Cosby Show* has succeeded spectacularly in both of its objectives. Through new forms of representation of black people, the show seems to be breaking down racist attitudes and opinions among white viewers. At the same time, this is not achieved by presenting an implausible picture of black life. Black audiences are attracted to it precisely because television is offering for the first time a picture of black life that they see as real.

We should caution the reader, however, against premature optimism. Our interviews also revealed *The Cosby Show* to be fostering other attitudes and perceptions that may lessen and even reverse the direction of the show's progressive movement. We believe, in fact, that *The Cosby Show* also has a profoundly negative influence on racial equality in American society. The roots of this problem lie not just with the show, but with the images of class that it reinforces. This argument has serious consequences for the whole debate about stereotyping on television, and the remainder of this book is therefore devoted to it.

4

Black Experience:
Images, Illusions,
and Social Class

GLORIA (*to Edith*):
"You've never told us how you feel about black people?"

EDITH BUNKER:
"Well, you sure gotta hand it to 'em. I mean, two years ago they were nothing but servants and janitors. Now they're teachers and doctors and lawyers. They've sure come a long way on TV."

—dialogue from TV sit-com *All in the Family*

The Cosby Show is part of a more general shift in the representation of black people on television in the United States. Spurred by the demands for "positive images" of minorities, the TV networks have been increasingly inclined to incorporate African Americans into the succession of cozy middle class households that parade across our TV screens.

Although a number of commentators have remarked upon this televisual trend toward black upward mobility, the extent of the change has not as yet been quantified. This is partly because measuring social class on television is extremely difficult: TV characters do not come handily classified in terms of income, occupation, and education. The social class of a character is often something we can only surmise on the basis of their general occupation or lifestyle, an inevitably imprecise procedure that makes any systematic content analysis tricky.

TABLE 4.1   The Social Class of TV Characters (in percent)

	Clearly Upper	Middle	Clearly Lower
1971–1976	8	88	4
1984–1989	9	90	1

BLACK IMAGES: THE CASE OF THE
DISAPPEARING BLACK WORKING CLASS

With that cautionary note, we shall sketch out the overall picture of black representation on North American television. Against this background, *The Cosby Show* can be seen to be part of a more general pattern.

Our data come from two sources. The historical analysis is drawn from the Cultural Indicators Project at the Annenberg School in Philadelphia, which has monitored the content of prime-time television for the past two decades. These data are supplemented by our own analysis of the content of one week of prime-time television broadcasting in November 1990.

To get a general picture of the class position of black and white people on television, we decided to compare two six-year periods (both periods come after the heyday of the Civil Rights movement, which made TV producers more sensitive to the cruder forms of racial stereotyping). The first, 1971 to 1976, is from what we might call the pre-Cosby era; the second, 1984 to 1989, marks the first half of what Henry Louis Gates has called "the Cosby decade."

The samples from the two periods consist of 2,081 major TV characters from the pre-Cosby era and 1,156 major TV characters from the Cosby period. These characters were all coded in terms of their race and social class. Social class is specified in three broad categories: upper middle or upper class, middle class, and working or lower class.

Table 4.1 shows that the vast majority of TV characters are middle class and that few are identifiably working class. Indeed, major blue-collar characters would appear to be a dying breed, down from 4 percent in the early 1970s to less than 1 percent in the late 1980s (in contrast to upper class characters, who slightly increased).

As we might expect, the overall percentage of black characters increased between the two periods, from 7 to 10 percent. The more dramatic change, however, is in their relative social status. Table 4.2 tallies class breakdown by race, showing that between the two periods working class black TV characters have experienced significant upward mobility.

Whereas 16 percent of black characters were working class in the pre-Cosby era, there were none at all in the Cosby period. Putting it another

TABLE 4.2 Changes in Distribution by Race and Class of TV Characters, 1971–1989, in percent

	Clearly Upper	Middle	Clearly Lower
1971–1976			
White	8	89	3
Black	2	82	16
1984–1989			
White	9.5	90	0.5
Black	4	96	0

way, 30 percent of the working class characters on television between 1971 and 1976 were black; between 1984 and 1989, none of them were. The black working class seems to have disappeared from our screens.

We can clarify this picture by looking at the more detailed 1990 sample. This sample consisted of 116 minority characters, of whom 106 were black (despite the large and growing Hispanic population in the United States, only 4 percent of minority characters were Hispanic).

The sample was divided fairly evenly between major and minor characters (52 percent major, 48 percent minor), usually appearing in drama series (49 percent) or sitcoms (41 percent). We tried to be fairly specific about each character's social class, combining information about occupation with life-style and other social indicators. At the top of the scale, upper middle class refers to high-income professionals (well-established doctors, lawyers, or business executives); at the bottom of the scale we included an "underclass" category to incorporate the various lower class crooks that appeared in a number of shows. The final category is for those it was impossible to categorize.

Among the black characters, the social class breakdown (in percent) was as follows:

Underclass	10
Working class	7
Lower middle class	15
Middle class	35
Upper middle class	26
Unclear	7

Once again, we can see that black TV characters tend to occupy positions at the higher end of the social scale. Furthermore, a number of working class characters came from an episode of the series *Quantum Leap*, which was set in the early days of the Civil Rights movement. *Quantum Leap* was one of only two programs that dealt with racism and the only one

TABLE 4.3 Major and Minor TV Characters by Class, 1990 (in percent)

	Major	*Minor*
Underclass	12	13
Working class	2	14
Lower middle class	15	13
Middle class	28	41
Upper middle class	38	11
Unclear	5	8

to do so explicitly. The general pattern on television consigns black working class people to history.

When characters from the lower end of the social scale do appear, they are more likely to be crooks than car workers, more often social deviants than secretaries. This is in part due to the high number of drama series featuring elements of the criminal justice system (usually revolving around cops or lawyers). In fact, even in shows that had nothing to do with cops and robbers, the legal system was well represented: Nearly a third (31 percent) of the characters in our sample were criminals, cops, detectives, lawyers, or judges.

As Table 4.3 shows, minority characters at the lower end of the social scale are less likely to play major roles. What is remarkable about this comparison is that, among major minority characters, upper middle class people outnumber ordinary working class people 19 to 1.

We can draw two fairly clear conclusions from these content studies. The first is that African Americans have been the beneficiaries of significant upward mobility on television. In the early 1970s, black people were proportionately much more likely to play working class characters than white people. Today, the comparative social status of black and white people appears to be almost indistinguishable. The second is that although upper middle class black characters have become fairly commonplace, working class blacks (particularly those in major roles) are rare on television.

As readers will be aware, these are not the only images of blacks on U.S. television. The story on television news is very different. Here, traditional stereotyping is still prevalent. As noted black writer Ishmael Reed (1991) has argued, black people are disproportionately likely to be portrayed as criminal on network news. For instance, though polls suggest that only 15 percent of drug users are black, network news stories associate drugs with blacks 50 percent of the time. As we will show later, many black people are aware of these disparities. Indeed, there has been a call (from Ishmael Reed and others) for a boycott of network news to protest the distortions.

Robert Entman (1990: 342), in a detailed analysis, has confirmed the existence of these disparities. In so doing he also discovered that African Americans are further symbolically removed from the "normal" community by being represented as a "special interest group."

> In the stories analyzed, crime reporting made blacks look particularly threatening, while coverage of politics exaggerated the degree to which black politicians (as compared with white ones) practice special interest politics.

Thus two very different and conflicting stories are being told on television about black people. We cannot assume that audiences, particularly white audiences, are aware of the contradiction. Moreover, as Entman himself suggests, it is a contradiction that creates a new set of disturbing racial beliefs.

BLACK REALITY: THE PERMANENT UNDERCLASS AND INCREASING POVERTY

We are used to the idea that television, though it may not be a mirror of society, does reflect basic social changes. How far, then, does television's portrayal of African Americans reflect real social trends? If the 1980s saw the spectacular success of the black middle class on prime-time television, what was the black experience in real life?

Once we turn off the TV and switch to social reality, the picture of black American life is rather bleak, especially for the millions trapped in the ghetto underclass. Looking at the ten-year period from 1975 to 1984, *The Economic Report of the People* (Center for Popular Economics, 1986: 44) shows that, far from improving, the economic position of black people has significantly declined overall. Although overall black family income has always been less than white family income, in the ten-year period under consideration it declined from 61 to 56 percent. Similarly, although the ratio of nonwhite unemployment to white unemployment has always been high, in the period from 1975 to 1984 it rose from 1.8:1 to 2.2:1. These figures indicate a reversal in some of the advances that black Americans made in the 1960s.

A similar story is revealed by census data reported in the U.S. Department of Commerce's *Statistical Abstract of the United States* (1990). As Table 4.4 shows, in the period from 1980 to 1988 there was a marked increase in black poverty, median black family income actually decreased, and fewer black families owned the homes in which they lived.

The most revealing figure perhaps is the 33 percent of black families that live below the poverty level. Most that live above this level live on modest working class incomes. Thus the Huxtables' lifestyle reflects the

TABLE 4.4   Income, Housing, and Race (in percent)

Family Income ($)	White		Black	
	1980	1988	1980	1988
Up to 4,999	2.4	3.2	9.7	13.5
5,000–9,999	6.0	6.1	17.7	16.5
10,000–14,999	8.4	8.6	14.6	12.5
15,000–24,999	19.5	18.4	21.7	21.8
25,000–34,999	20.0	18.1	15.3	13.6
35,000–49,999	23.0	21.2	13.0	12.8
Over 50,000	20.8	24.4	7.9	9.5
Median income	$30,669	$30,853	$18,122	$18,098
Below poverty line	9.0	10.5	31.0	33.1
Home owners	70.5	67.2	48.6	42.4
Renters	27.7	31.0	49.6	55.7

Source: From U.S. Department of Commerce, *Statistical Abstract of the United States 1990,* table 43.

reality of only a small minority of black families. The great majority of black families, in income and housing, are at the other end of the socioeconomic spectrum—and the 1980s have seen a general reversal in the economic well-being of black Americans.

Many more statistics reveal the declining fortunes of black Americans, particularly in the Reagan-Bush years, but statistics alone do not tell the whole gloomy story of the millions of black Americans who live in the inner-city ghettos. Characterized by extreme poverty, serious and violent crime, high rates of drug addiction, permanent joblessness and welfare dependency, and dramatic increases in out-of-wedlock births and female-headed families, the central core of many American cities has been converted into a no-go area that requires constant police occupation. William Julius Wilson in his definitive books *The Declining Significance of Race* and *The Truly Disadvantaged* discusses this situation as the "problems of social dislocation in the inner city" (1987: 22). In what follows we draw heavily on Wilson's analysis.

Although only 1 out of 9 people in the United States is black, in 1984 nearly 50 percent of those arrested for murder and nonnegligent manslaughter were black, and 41 percent of all murder victims were black. Homicide is the leading cause of death for black Americans aged 25 to 34. North American manufacturing may not be what it once was, but when it comes to incarcerating its citizens, the United States leads the world (locking up 426 people per 100,000). In the United States, prison populations are swollen with disproportionate numbers of young black men, the majority of them from the inner-city ghettos. The number of black men between the ages of 20 and 29 in prison is greater than the number of all black men in college (all data are from the *Guardian Weekly,* June 30, 1991, 10). Some commentators have referred to these statistics as indicating the creation of a growing American gulag, where the majority of inmates are blacks or other minorities.

For black, inner-city males not in prison, the chances of gaining lawful employment are not very good. William Julius Wilson (1987: 42–43) writes:

> Heavily concentrated in central cities, blacks have experienced a deterioration of their economic position on nearly all the major labor-market indicators. . . . Blacks, especially young males, are dropping out of the labor force in significant numbers. . . . The percentage of black males in the labor force fell sharply between 1960 and 1984 for those aged sixteen to twenty-four, and somewhat less for those aged twenty-five to thirty-four. . . . Only a minority of noninstitutionalized black youth are employed. . . . The percentage of black male youth who are employed has sharply and steadily decreased since 1955, whereas among white males it has increased only slightly for all categories. The fact that only 58 percent of all black young adult males, 34 percent of all black males aged eighteen to nineteen, and 16 percent of those aged sixteen to seventeen were employed in 1984 reveals a problem of joblessness for young black men that has reached catastrophic proportions.

The absence of young black males through incarceration and the growing rate of their unemployment are closely connected to other characteristics of the current inner city: the dramatic increase in black out-of-wedlock births and the rise in the number of female-headed families. Sociologists see these as indications of a serious transformation (and breakdown) of established family structures. Although female-headed households generally increased by 51 percent between 1974 and 1984, among blacks and Hispanics the increase was extraordinary. The number of families headed by white women grew by 63 percent, but the number of families headed by black women grew by 108 percent. Wilson argues that although numerous interacting factors account for these patterns, the single most important cause of the rise of black female-headed families is not the often-quoted attraction of welfare but the problem of black male joblessness (because marriage is closely linked with finding a marriage partner having stable employment).

The rise of female-headed families has had "dire social and economic consequences because these families are far more vulnerable to poverty than are other types of families. Indeed, sex and marital status of the head are the most important determinants of poverty status for families, especially in urban areas" (Wilson, 1987: 71). Moreover, female-headed families are far more likely than male-headed families to be persistently poor.

The inner city has become a social and economic disaster area, with high rates of violent crime, unemployment, and persistent poverty. The response of the country's leaders to this appalling reality has been to contain the problem rather than to confront it. For most of America's leaders, the problems of the inner city can be disregarded as long as they remain *in* the inner city, well away from the comfortable suburban enclaves. White America has created its own class of untouchables, out of sight and out of mind. The human wasteland created by years of social and economic neglect is seen only as a law-and-order problem. This myopia is fed by a self-interested, suburbanite mentality, for which an army of unemployed blacks is a problem only if it creeps into other neighborhoods and robs people. The major vehicle for dealing with the inner city in the last twenty years has therefore been an increased police occupation force, which channels young black males into a crowded and violent prison system. The result has been the establishment of a permanent black ghetto underclass.

THE RACE-CLASS NEXUS

Even if most people would rather not think about it, the story we have told is fairly well known. Finding solutions to the problems of joblessness and crime requires that we understand how the situation arose. To understand the present overall situation of African Americans, as Wilson has argued, there needs to be a switch in focus from race-based explanations to class-based explanations. (In what follows we use a relatively simple notion of class: the socioeconomic, material, and cultural conditions in which people live.)

Wilson identifies three distinct periods of race relations in the United States. The first is the *preindustrial,* coinciding with antebellum slavery and the postbellum era. The second is the *industrial* period, which lasts from the end of the nineteenth century to the New Deal era. Both periods were characterized by explicit efforts by whites to solidify economic racial domination "through various forms of juridical, political and social discrimination" (Wilson, 1980: 4). State and federal government policies were overtly directed against the black population and were justified by a system of racial beliefs based on assumptions of black biological and cultural inferiority.

In the third, the *modern industrial,* period the political system, responding to varying degrees of black political pressure, "has tended to promote racial equality" (Wilson, 1980: 17). Even conservative presidents like Reagan and Bush have been forced to speak the words of racial equality (and in President Reagan's case forced to sign into law a national holiday commemorating the Rev. Martin Luther King, Jr.). Wilson argues that through a mixture of political and economic changes, it is no longer racism that explains the life chances of blacks; instead it is their class position. We will attempt to demonstrate how this shift occurred by examining the conditions that led to the emergence of a black middle class and the establishment of a black ghetto underclass.

The industrial period of race relations is characterized by the migration of southern blacks into northern industrial urban centers, where they were segregated into discrete neighborhoods. As a result of this segregation, a black middle class developed to service needs of the black population that were not met by white middle class professionals. "The black doctor, lawyer, teacher, minister, businessman, mortician, excluded from the white community, was able to create a niche in the segregated black community" (Wilson, 1980: 20). Discriminated against in housing and employment, the new black middle class lived in the same neighborhoods as their working class patrons and clients—the inner city.

The inner city has not always been the disaster area it is today. Though it suffered from poverty, the inner city's rates of unemployment, violent crime, and female-headed families were much lower. Wilson (1987: 3) writes that in the 1940s residents of Harlem and other ghetto neighborhoods slept outside on fire escapes or rooftops on hot summer nights, that whites frequented inner-city bars and clubs, and that "unlike the present period, inner-city communities prior to 1960 exhibited the features of social organization—including a sense of community, positive neighborhood identification, and explicit norms and sanctions against aberrant behavior."

Economic, demographic, and political changes in the postwar period created the ground for new kinds of shifts. First, the factory-based economy of the inner city was dispersed to the outskirts as improvements in communication and transportation made it more feasible to use cheap, open tracts of land. And "traditional central-city multistory factories have been rendered obsolete with the introduction and diffusion of single-level assembly line modes of production" (Wilson, 1980: 93). This resulted not so much in the loss of industry for the inner city but in a lack of industrial growth and expansion and limited opportunities for persons entering the work force in the inner cities.

At the same time, the economy was also starting to shift from a manufacturing base to the proliferation of service industries, resulting in a rapid expansion of white-collar jobs that required relatively higher levels of education for entry. The relocation of industry to the suburbs coupled with the shift in need from low-skilled, undereducated to high-skilled, well-educated workers crippled the inner-city economies. The situation was made even worse by a growth in absolute numbers of black teenagers just as employment opportunities were shrinking. Wilson (1980: 97) writes:

> In the face of the decreasing demand for labor and the more rigorous prerequisites for higher levels of employment, teenagers and other workers entering the labor market for the first time find it increasingly difficult to obtain employment in the corporate sector. Blacks constitute a sizable percentage of both corporate sector workers who have become redundant because of advancing technology and the new job-seekers locked out of this sector of the economy.

However, not all sectors of the black population have suffered as a result of these changes. The black middle classes, through a mixture of economic and political factors, have been able to take advantage of the opportunities created by the new situation.

On the whole, it was the black middle class that set the agenda for the Civil Rights movement of the 1960s; and it was the freedoms they were most interested in—to attend schools of their choice, to swim in certain swimming pools, to eat in restaurants of their choice, to be able to attend any movie theater, to have the same voting privileges as whites— that came to define their goals. As Wilson (1980: 21) says, "These basic concerns were reflected in the 1964 Civil Rights Bill which helped to create the illusion that when the needs of the black middle class were met, so were the needs of the entire black community." Tragically, when Martin Luther King, Jr., started to talk about widening the economic goals of the struggle, and when Malcolm X started to recognize that poor blacks shared much in common with poor whites, they were both murdered.

The expansion of the white-collar sector (both private and governmental), along with affirmative action programs prompted by rising black political power, provided opportunities for higher-educated middle class blacks to get better paying jobs and to move out of the segregated inner city. As Wilson (1987: 147) writes:

> The competitive resources developed by the *advantaged minority members*— resources that flow directly from the family stability, schooling, income, and peer groups that their parents have been able to provide—result in their benefiting disproportionately from policies that promote the rights of minority individuals by removing artificial barriers to valued positions.

Affirmative action programs, in other words, have helped relatively few black people. They have had almost no impact upon lower class blacks.

Indeed their impact on lower class blacks could be said to be entirely negative, for as the black middle class was able to leave its inner-city homelands, it took with it the institutions that were needed to sustain community life.

Wilson (1987: 144) argues that the stable black working class that was qualified for the new, skilled, manufacturing jobs and the black middle class provided a "social buffer" for the poorer sections of the black population:

> The basic thesis is not that ghetto culture went unchecked following the removal of higher-income families in the inner city, but that the removal of these families made it more difficult to sustain the basic institutions in the inner city (including churches, stores, schools, recreational facilities, etc.) in the face of prolonged joblessness. And as the basic institutions declined, the social organization of inner-city neighborhoods (defined here to include a sense of community, positive neighborhood identification, and explicit norms and sanctions against aberrant behavior) likewise declined.

These movements went hand in hand with and contributed to the fiscal crisis of the inner cities. As industries moved and took with them the highest paid residents, the income and property tax base collapsed (at the same time that more and more young people were unemployed and needed increased social services). The spiraling situation is most apparent in education, where the population of undersupported urban public schools is becoming increasingly black as well as lower class. "The children who have the greatest need for education are receiving the poorest training" (Wilson, 1980: 114), thereby being trapped in the ghetto even more tightly. The only choice after school is welfare or crime. The more the situation deteriorates, the more rapidly anyone who can afford to move leaves. "Accordingly, the flight to the suburbs of the more affluent families has meant that the central cities are increasingly becoming the domain of the poor and the stable working class" (Wilson, 1980: 115).

Not all sectors of the black population are suffering in the same way. Indeed, in the last twenty years, the black middle class has done quite well. It is therefore difficult to argue that the plight of the black underclass is a consequence solely of racial oppression. If this were so, we would expect all black people, regardless of class, to have been equally disadvantaged. We can now begin to understand that it is a racially inflected class structure that has placed lower class blacks in the most disadvantaged position to compete in the present economy. As Wilson (1980: 23) sums up:

For in a very real sense, the current problems of lower-class blacks are substantially related to fundamental structural changes in the economy. A history of discrimination and oppression created a huge black underclass, and the technological and economic revolutions have combined to ensure it a permanent status. . . . In the modern industrial period fundamental economic and political changes have made economic class position more important than race in determining black chances for occupational mobility.

CLASS AND SOCIAL MOBILITY

Our discussion in this chapter of "the declining significance of race" should not be taken to mean that we believe racism to have been eradicated in the United States. We do not. Rather, we are arguing that the chances (or lack of them) for black upward mobility must be understood within a framework of contemporary class relations. The significant differences within the black population make it meaningless to talk in terms of race alone. Only within a class framework can we make sense of the existence and the fortunes of a black middle class, a black working class, and a large, permanent, black underclass.

Although "official" racial barriers may have diminished, class barriers may prove to be just as unpassable for the large majority of black people— just as they are unpassable for a majority of white people. The fact of huge disparities in income is characteristic of the type of industrialized market society (capitalism) that we live in. There is no doubting that in the contest for economic advancement, different people start with very different kinds of resources. The official mythology of our society, the so-called American dream, does not deny this. It simply states that the playing field is level, that although everyone may not start with the same income and wealth, everyone has the same chance to reach the top of the income hierarchy because a person's class background does not limit a person's chances of economic success. Though fanciful, this belief is a significant framework within which we think about our society. Although everyone knows and accepts that there is no equality of *income,* it is also accepted that there is equality of *opportunity.*

Social reality does not match the dream, yet the majority of people still believe it. This delusion is encouraged by a media system that propagates the myth by showing us people who have made it from nothing, by turning the "exceptions" into the "rule." This hides the true structural barriers to intergenerational social mobility.

There are at least three different ways in which class background (normally the socioeconomic position of the family into which one is born) structures one's life chances. The first important source of inequality of opportunity is the intergenerational transmission of wealth, whereby parents pass on wealth to their children. Wealthier parents provide more wealth to their children, adding to their chances of economic success, than do poorer parents.

A second aspect of unequal opportunity concerns the transmission from parents to children of the capacity to command income. Parents can assure that their children are prepared to enter the labor market most advantageously by supplying them, for instance, with the highest possible level of education. Economist Sam Bowles (1986) has demonstrated how the jobs people have are related to the duration and quality of their education and how the level and quality of a child's education are related to the socioeconomic position of parents. Bowles (1986: 240, 243) concludes:

> In an advanced capitalist society in which education and skills play an important role in the hierarchy of production, then, laws guaranteeing inheritance are not enough to reproduce the social division of labor from generation to generation. Skills and educational credentials must somehow be passed on within the family. . . . Schools play an important part in reproducing and legitimizing this modern form of class structure. . . . The argument that our "egalitarian" education compensates for inequalities generated elsewhere in the capitalist system is patently fallacious.

Although the first two aspects of unequal opportunity relate to what has been called "economic capital" (what wealth buys), the third aspect refers to what the French sociologist Pierre Bourdieu calls "cultural capital." This refers to the "training" provided within the family about good taste, good manners, ways of interacting, and ways of thinking. Again Sam Bowles argues that there is a relationship between class position and class culture and that wealthier classes are better able to prepare their children to attain higher positions in the social division of labor by encouraging independence, self-reliance, and other traits that have been labeled as valuable within the economic hierarchy. "The operation of the labor market," argues Bowles (1986: 245), "translates differences in class culture into income inequalities and occupational hierarchies. The personality traits, values, and expectations characteristic of different class cultures play a major role in determining an individual's success in gaining a higher income or prestigious occupation."

We have talked a great deal in this chapter about the influence of social class. To have an adequate understanding of how American society works, it is necessary (though certainly not sufficient) to be able to see how class acts as one structuring aspect. Without such a framework, we are unable to address why certain groups and individuals do systematically better than others.

In a recent and timely book, cultural critic Benjamin DeMott (1990: 9) has argued, rightly in our view, that America "can't think straight about class" because it is "a nation in shackles, its thought, character, and public policy locked in distortion and lies. . . . Several hallowed concepts—independence, individualism, choice—are woven into this web of illusion and self-deception. But presiding over the whole stands the icon of *classlessness*." American society, in other words, does not have a way of talking about one of its central organizing features, yet it is something that everyone intuitively knows exists and is important.

Stanley Aronowitz (1989) contends that these necessary discussions have been displaced in popular culture onto gender relations. Commenting on recent films, he states that much of what passes for gender relations is a displaced form of class discourse. The same thing, we shall argue, could be said about race. People substitute racial categories for class categories—hence the accusation sometimes leveled at middle class blacks (like the Huxtables) that they have become "too white."

In the chapters that follow we look carefully at how both white and black audiences make sense of *The Cosby Show* regarding what it says about social mobility. We believe that Americans are unable to think clearly about race because they cannot think clearly about class. The increasing number of images of black upper middle class life, including and propelled by the Huxtables, do represent a reality of some sections of the black population. But they also crucially hide and distort how the majority of black Americans are understood. This distortion leads to the emergence of a new set of regressive racial beliefs. Behind these distortions and beliefs lies the myth of classlessness.

5

Class and the Myth
of the American Dream

We have detailed the disparity between the upwardly mobile position of black people on television and the acutely disadvantaged position of many black people in society. We have, thus far, concentrated on the positive consequences of this disparity, particularly the role played by positive TV images in countering traditional stereotypes of African Americans. In this chapter we begin to address some of the less sanguine consequences of this televisual distortion, which we find to be deeply disturbing.

MISREPRESENTATIONS AND MISCONCEPTIONS

The problem concerns the picture of the United States painted by *The Cosby Show* and goes beyond the series itself. It includes the more general trend that *The Cosby Show* has stimulated, a trend toward the proliferation of middle and upper middle class black characters on television. This trend is not the boost for positive race relations that it appears to be. Our evidence suggests, in fact, that the presence of these apparently benign images of black people on television constitutes, for African Americans, a serious step backward.

Our argument is, in essence, a simple one: programs like *The Cosby Show* encourage the viewer to see the real world through rose-tinted spectacles. As we suggested in Chapter 2, the viewers' ability to distinguish the TV world from the real one does not prevent them from confusing the two. *The Cosby Show,* we discovered, helps to cultivate an impression, particularly among white people, that racism is no longer a problem in the United States. Our audience study revealed that the overwhelming majority of white TV viewers felt racism was a sin of the past; *The Cosby*

Show, accordingly, represented a new "freedom of opportunity" apparently enjoyed by black people. If Cliff and Clair can make it, in other words, then so can all blacks. The positive images of blacks promoted by shows like *Cosby* have, therefore, distinctly negative consequences by creating a conservative and comfortable climate of opinion that allows white America to ignore widespread racial inequality.

The consequences of this misconception are profound, and we shall explore them in the chapters that follow. In this chapter, we shall address some of the attitudes, along with television's part in them, that allow such a misconception to develop. These attitudes, we shall suggest, have as much to do with class as with race.

TELEVISION AND THE "AMERICAN DREAM"

Thinking about racism in the United States has been muddled in the past few years because, although racial equality (in theory, at least) has been achieved politically, it has not been achieved economically. The economic system effectively subjugates most black people. African Americans, having been placed at the bottom of the economic pile, are forced to struggle against inequalities in material and educational resources. In the current economic and political system, few can win such a struggle. Free market capitalism, the organizing principle of this system, allows the United States to forgo racist principles while maintaining a degree of white hegemony, a lesson the white minority in Zimbabwe have, to their undoubted satisfaction, quickly learned.

It is useful to distinguish between two notions of racism. The first, which we have discussed, is based upon the operation of social structures in which privilege based on race is firmly inscribed (through a barrier-ridden class system). The second notion is very different. Such racism is based not on the functioning of social institutions but upon the behavior of individuals; it is, the theory goes, an interpersonal rather than a social problem. The drawback with the second theory is not that racism does not exist at an interpersonal level; it clearly does. The difficulty comes when we try to understand the reasons for racial distinctions in achievement and performance. If distinctions by race were simply a product of white people's racism in the school and the workplace, then a more liberal attitude among white people should herald the disappearance of those distinctions. This theory fails to appreciate how society actually works.

During our audience study, it became increasingly clear that the viewers' inability to perceive the growing racial distinctions in the United States was bound up with an unawareness of the limiting effects of a class system. Most people in our survey saw racism firmly within the confines of individualism. It is not simply that they were unable to draw connections between race and class; they found it difficult to talk about the social effects of class at all, confirming DeMott's thesis summarized in the previous chapter.

What role does television play in this ideological process? The answer, suggested by the group discussions, is that television envisages class not as a series of barriers but as a series of hurdles that can be overcome. That view promotes the idea of the American dream. Although the American dream was not invented for television, television appears to nourish and sustain it. We see countless examples of people making it, but few examples of people (apart from the lazy, deviant, or generally undeserving) *prevented* from making it. This makes it easy for us to think of the individual enterprise that defines the American dream as the organizing principle of the social structure—and difficult for us to conceive or articulate the idea of *in*equality of opportunity.

The Cosby Show, by incorporating a black family into the American dream, plays an important part in this ideological process. It symbolizes the fairness of the American system. The fact that the Huxtables are an African American family is central to this process: their success assures us that in the United States everyone, regardless of race or creed, can enjoy material success.

The American dream that *The Cosby Show* promotes is built on the cracks in an otherwise fairly solid class system, which ensures that most poor people will stay poor and most rich people will stay rich, in cycles that inexorably revolve from one generation to the next. The system is not, however, inexorable: the cracks in it may be too small to threaten its survival, but they are large enough to allow a few people to slip upward. These happy few are seen as confirming the American dream, whose strange logic transforms them from exceptions to the rule, creating the idea that there are, in fact, *no* rules.

The ideological power of the American dream involves more than the distortion of social reality. Mark Crispin Miller describes the Huxtable home as "the corporate showcase" that displays both the availability and the desirability of "the American Dream" (Miller, 1986: 210). It is, in other words, a dream that speaks to us not only about what is possible but what is desirable. The Huxtables' upper middle class life-style is dangled before us as an image of not only what we could have but what we *should* have. Here is the comfortable world of nice cars, kitchen gadgets, and designer clothes—go for it! As one respondent put it:

> *I think they're holding this family up as a role model and something to aspire to, to have smart kids and lead a nice life, and get along well with your family, and enjoy each other; and it really is a very,*

very strong role model to aspire to. I think this is what they're trying to do . . . and still at the same time be very, very human, having the same problems as anybody else.

The American dream is not an innocent ideological notion. To sustain consent for a market economy constructed upon enormous disparities in income and wealth, it is necessary to persuade people not to question but to consume. People need to be convinced that, regardless of their circumstances, the system is fundamentally fair. If at the same time they can be encouraged to maximize their consumer spending, so much the better. We should realize, in this sense, that the American dream plays neatly into the hands of those promoting unfettered free market capitalism. However encouraging and hopeful the American dream may be, it sustains a right-wing political agenda.

Although this view of the world did not originate in North American TV programs, it is an attitude that they continually cultivate and sustain. As we suggested in Chapter 2, television fiction in the United States is distinctly skewed in favor of middle and upper middle class characters. In the TV world, normality is attached to being comfortably middle class, being average means being above average. To be outside this world is, by implication, to be out of the mainstream, marginal, and, in a socioeconomic sense, conspicuously unsuccessful. This economically elevated televisual world encourages TV programs like *The Cosby Show* to conform to its rules and to assume that acceptance into the mainstream involves being privileged.

Television, in the United States, combines an implicit endorsement of certain middle class life-styles with a squeamish refusal to confront class realities or class issues. This is neither inevitable nor natural. Nothing about being working or lower middle class prevents someone from being funny, proud, dignified, entertaining, or worthy of admiration and respect, even if the social setting of most TV programs would encourage you to believe otherwise.

On British television, for example, some of the most popular shows are based upon working class characters in predominantly working class communities. The two most enduringly popular British TV series, *East-enders* and *Coronation Street,* take place in the working class districts of, respectively, East London and Salford (near Manchester), and a host of other popular shows, from *Minder* to *Only Fools and Horses,* revolve around unambiguously working class characters. Class differences and class conflicts (rarely seen on U.S. television) are constantly found interwoven in the dramatic action, whether as a source of humor or a source of tension.

These characteristics are not typical, significantly enough, of most British programs that make their way across the Atlantic (usually to be shown on PBS). Most working class characters (unless they are of the quaint variety found on programs like *Upstairs, Downstairs*) get mysteriously lost along the way. The irony of this pattern of selection is that it leads many people in the United States to suppose that U.S. TV programs are more relevant than British TV programs to the lives of ordinary people.

There are exceptions, of course, on the U.S. side, of which *Roseanne* is the best known recent example. The audience reaction to *Roseanne*, from within our survey and elsewhere, is extremely revealing. The series centers on the lives of an ordinary working class family; because it does so, it is perceived not as ordinary but unusual. It is clearly identified as offering TV viewers something different. When our audience members were asked about working class people on television, many spontaneously mentioned *Roseanne*. In a TV world populated by middle class families on shows like *The Cosby Show, Family Ties, Growing Pains, Fresh Prince, Doogie Howser,* and *The Wonder Years, Roseanne* is notable for this very reason.

What makes *Roseanne* even more unusual is that it occasionally offers viewers glimpses of the class barriers that stand in the way of working families like the Connors (in *Roseanne*). In some episodes, we are offered the notions not only that life is tougher for working class people but that things in the United States are neither equal nor fair. In one episode, Roseanne is in the local IRS office, trying, along with many other people, to sort out some confusion about her tax form. After being given a hard time by an impatient official, she loudly denounces the system, which, she declares (to the cheers of those around her) only offers breaks and loopholes to the rich, requiring ordinary people to carry their full burden.

This is, in the world of television, a rare glimpse at the oppressive side of a class system. We are more used to seeing class issues treated in other ways on prime-time television. When class barriers are presented, it is invariably to show them being overcome, not reinforced. This leads working class and middle class audiences to watch television very differently.

CLASS CONSCIOUSNESS: THE VIEW FROM ABOVE

Even in the simple act of watching television, the ideological effect of the American dream, for all its democratic rhetoric, is anything but egalitarian. It offers wealthier citizens the comfort and satisfaction of feeling included but forces poorer people to denigrate their own lot, and ultimately, to denigrate themselves for having failed. It is, however, within these limited ideological parameters that most people in our study spoke about class. The way we see class on television, in other words, depends on the class position we are watching from.

All our groups were asked, for example, how they would feel if *The Cosby Show* were about a lower middle class or blue-collar family. Though many respondents, particularly whites, responded negatively to the idea, a few actually embraced it. We might expect such a reaction from middle class viewers, but we might have anticipated a rather different response from the working class groups, who would, after all, have more in common with a less affluent family. Although middle class viewers enjoyed seeing themselves reflected on the screen, most working class or lower middle class viewers simply did not want to see a family that was, in a material sense, more like them.

The viewers in the best position to regard an upper middle class family like the Huxtables as normal and typical are, of course, those from middle or upper middle class backgrounds. Such respondents, as one might expect, clearly enjoyed the ease with which they felt able to identify with or relate to the show. When offered the prospect of transforming the Huxtables into a blue-collar family, most responded uncomfortably. As one respondent put it, far better to keep it "sophisticated" and "select," to watch what another referred to as "classy" people. Black upper middle class viewers, as one might expect, had a particular stake in the show's portrayal of black professionals (which we discuss in more detail in Chapter 7). More prosperous white groups, for their own reasons, also expressed doubt about the prospects for a blue-collar *Cosby Show,* as this respondent did:

> *I don't think it would be funnier. I think it would probably be less funny [because] I think it's just a higher level of humor and situations than the other shows.*

For these white respondents, this class preference was not simply a question of money; it involved a level of cultural competence (or "sophistication") that is understood as class related. Most were shy about stating this point too explicitly, preferring to talk about the things they have in common with the Huxtables, as in the following exchange:

> MAN: *I think I enjoy the program more because he is a doctor, she is a professional.*
>
> WOMAN: *Identifying . . .*
>
> MAN: *We're both professionals. Our kids are going to go to college, their kids go to college.*

WOMAN: *It's just the situations.*

MAN: *For me, watching the program, I enjoy it more.*

WOMAN: *I can identify.*

MAN: *Because they're kind of like me!*

INTERVIEWER: *And you feel the same way?*

WOMAN: *Sure, I think it's just a higher level of humor and situations than the other shows.*

MAN: *That's right!*

Class is understood as more than an economic category; it is the expression of a number of cultural practices that middle and upper middle class audiences feel they share with the Huxtables. These practices incorporate everything from going to college to the "higher level of humor and situations" these respondents associate with class position.

Another respondent makes the same point rather more explicitly, using *Roseanne* and *The Cosby Show* to symbolize class distinction:

> *I don't know. I mean, I've turned* Roseanne *on, and I cannot get into that show at all. How it's popular is beyond my understanding. And I'm afraid that if you took this [Huxtable] family down to this level, in terms of their working class strata, then the humor would be like* Roseanne. *Because what happens when you work in a factory? What do people talk about? I mean, you know, for one day of my life I worked in the kitchen of a nursing home, and the humor was so awful, and I was sixteen years old, that I did not go back. Do you know what I am saying? It was just something I could not relate to at all.*

Although this respondent's class consciousness is reflected in the other upper middle class discussions, few were so explicit in articulating their distaste for working class culture.

The use of *Roseanne* as a cultural symbol is, in this respect, particularly interesting. *Roseanne*, we have suggested, was repeatedly identified by respondents, black as well as white, as a conspicuously "working class" sitcom. It follows that the middle class respondents responding positively to the Huxtables' class position would, like the respondent quoted above, find a working class sitcom like *Roseanne* not at all to their taste, as another middle class respondent made clear:

Sometimes I can watch it [Roseanne] and sometimes I just can't look at them, you know, I mean watch it. The house is a mess and I just can't deal with it. . . . I just don't like the way they look.

Some middle class respondents, however, confounded the logic of this position and responded positively to both *Roseanne* and *The Cosby Show*. This response suggests an intermingling of perceptions of class and race. To the middle class white audience, the Huxtables' class position is more important than the Connors'. To make the Huxtables working class would push them toward the cultural world inhabited by other, more working class black sitcoms (like *Good Times* or *The Jeffersons*), a cultural territory these respondents uniformly rejected. This phenomenon has different roots for black and white audiences, which we explore further in the next two chapters.

Whether they like *Roseanne* or not, the white middle and upper middle class groups credit *The Cosby Show* with a cultural value that is explicitly class related. As this group member put it:

I think class is important. Definitely. I think that class is all-important in the show. They're educated professionals. If they were working class, the situations that they would be showing would be very different.

Another group interpreted the Huxtables' aesthetic tastes directly in class terms: If they were lower middle or working class, "you wouldn't expect them to be so cultured," able to "afford the finer things in life" such as "the artwork, the jazz clubs, and I think I remember something about an auction or something where they got that painting." Although some of the black groups interpreted these symbols as signifying African-American culture, to the middle and upper middle class white audience they represent something different: they are a source of cultural identification based on class rather than race.

Television's celebration of middle and upper middle class lifestyles is, therefore, not simply a source of self-gratification for wealthier viewers; it allows them to develop a class consciousness that separates them from the less sophisticated hordes beneath them. It is their "cultured" knowledge and appreciation of "the finer things in life" that make them conscious of their membership in a privileged class. You are included in this world, television tells these viewers, because you deserve to be.

CLASS CONSCIOUSNESS: THE VIEW FROM BELOW

In the face of the cultural exclusivity identified by their wealthier counterparts, how is it that the white working class and lower middle class audiences were able to identify with the Huxtables, to categorize them, as many did, as "typical" and "average," as "a regular family, having the same problems just like us"? This question is particularly pertinent for white working class viewers, who cannot feel any identification based on class *or* race. The answer, in short, is that although *The Cosby Show* encourages class consciousness in middle class viewers, it dissolves it for the working class audience. As the interviews make clear, this is a necessary condition for the show's popularity among this audience. Although a class conscious response makes middle class viewers feel included, it would make less affluent viewers feel decidedly excluded.

Most lower middle and working class viewers were able to articulate a separation—one that the more affluent respondents were unable to make—between cultural competence and social class. The Huxtables' class position is, in economic terms, undisputed. In a cultural sense, however, it appears to be, for most working and lower middle class viewers, much more ambiguous. This ambiguity is partly the result of Bill Cosby's comic skill and his ability to focus on universal topics, a skill one respondent defined thus:

> *I think you see yourself in those positions the way that show is. It takes everyday life type of things and it's funny, because a lot of things that happen in everyday life are funny.*

This ingenious ambiguity allows the development of a discourse that identifies the Huxtables as upper middle class in a material rather than a cultural sense. They have the pleasures and comfort associated with wealth; yet their values and behavior make them "just a regular family." So, as one respondent put it, "They don't have the lifestyles you expect with the incomes they have; they keep themselves down to earth."

This idea was sometimes articulated by drawing comparisons with what were identified as negative aspects of upper middle class culture, which was characterized as "pseudo-intellectual" and difficult to relate to. As one man put it in relation to Cliff:

> *I guess he doesn't really seem professional, you know, not the way a doctor would be. Like when you go to doctor's office, it's totally different. . . . I work for the phone company and the ones I meet are very uppity and they really look down on the lower class.*

Most other white working class respondents echoed this sentiment, making it clear that there was little in a cultural sense to distinguish themselves from the Huxtables:

> *They don't play the status they are in the show. You know, he's a doctor, she's a lawyer—you'd expect them to be living a much higher class, flashing the money, but they're very down to earth, not flashing money around or anything like that. Maybe a lower class, maybe the background, the furniture, wouldn't be as nice, but I don't think it would change the characters at all.*

The middle and upper middle class respondents, predictably, included Bill Cosby within their own cultural milieu. This discourse allows working class and lower middle class respondents to do precisely the same thing.

It is a reading of the series that makes the possibility of upward mobility more conceivable because the Huxtables were, as one group put it, "role models" but "at the same time very human, having the same problems as everyone else." Upward mobility is defined in strictly economic, not cultural, terms, and the Huxtables' "down to earth quality" makes them an appropriate symbol, as one respondent put it, of "something to aspire to." One potentially upwardly mobile woman, referring to her friends in college, stated:

> *There's more business majors and there's more engineering majors and things like that, because they want to make a lot of money so that they can live like the Cosbys.*

What is perhaps most interesting about her comment is that she went on to lament this materialistic motive for going to college "so that you can get a good job . . . rather than to get a good education." The desire to "live like the Cosbys," in other words, is a purely economic rather than a cultural goal.

The educational and cultural competencies that support class barriers are thereby dissolved, the Huxtables being both wealthy and a "normal," "regular" family. Their wealth, in this sense, does not appear exclusive; rather it is something attainable by anyone. If the Huxtables were seen as upper middle class in a cultural sense, with values and concerns distinct to that lifestyle, working class viewers would feel excluded, and this would not be possible.

The Cosby Show, working within the ideology of the American dream, succeeds in having it both ways. Whether the viewer is close to the Huxtables' class position does not matter, because it is possible to view the Huxtables as reflecting the values of either position. Both audiences are able to identify with a program that, in the words of one respondent, "shows the best things about this country": for one audience because *The Cosby Show* is seen as "sophisticated" and "select," for the other because it is not. Class barriers (in the form of an upper middle class cultural elitism) are observed only by viewers unthreatened by those barriers. To everyone else, the show exhibits the universality of the American dream.

In the absence of more critical discourses of class or racial consciousness, this aspect of *The Cosby Show*'s ambiguity sustains the meritocratic mythology that allows the U.S. population to accept enormous differences in wealth. The show is, to some extent, forced into this logic by the language of mainstream television in the United States, where middle or upper middle class means normal. It is easier for *The Cosby Show* to have a broad appeal if it fits within the privileged confines of this world.

THE DISPLACEMENT OF CLASS
ONTO RACE

For black audiences this upward shift to the normality of the rest of prime-time fare comes with a built-in contradiction. Although the Huxtables may slide effortlessly into the world of TV sitcoms, they are, as an upper middle class family (a lawyer *and* a doctor!) fairly unusual. Only a tiny minority of black people in the United States live like the Huxtables. So, although nearly all black respondents praised *The Cosby Show* for its realism, at other times in the interviews they acknowledged that it portrayed a world that did not represent what they knew as "the black experience." The following comments were all made during discussions that generally approved of the Huxtables' status, but the contradictions involved were allowed to seep through:

> I would like to see racial issues. I would like to see prejudicial issues. And for me that's more the real world. It seems like it's almost a soap opera. They always have everything involved in their own little nest, in their own home. Nothing on the outside. . . . I would like to see them with some real crisis, real issues of "Well, Dad, hey, I went for a job and I got discriminated against."

> What I think they should do on the Cosby Show is make it to more where it's like . . . I mean it doesn't have to be all bad . . . like every week you hear something bad, but they never like, say, talk about the drugs, and they live in New York City and you don't ever hear them talking about drugs. . . . They never have problems like normal kids. . . . They never talk about the drug problem or problems among black people.

> I mean not every week, of course, but I'd like to see real-life crisis issues. I'd like to see Theo maybe get involved with a gang maybe. I'd like to see Theo maybe get involved with drugs or whatever.

In part this ambiguity is reflected in a feeling, based in real experience and knowledge, that there is a kind of contradiction between being "black" and being "middle class," that these are, in a cultural sense, mutually exclusive categories. There is, after all, a clear correlation between race and class: black people are much more likely to be working class or poor than white people, while the emergence of a black upper middle class is a fairly recent phenomenon. Accordingly, the portrayal of people like the Huxtables means negotiating new cultural territory, a territory infused with complex assumptions about what it is to be black in the United States.

What is notable about our black focus groups' responses is not what was said but what remained unsaid. Just as most white respondents found it difficult to talk about class issues, so did black respondents. Though this difficulty led both sets of respondents to similar understandings or misunderstandings about the world, some of its consequences are quite specific. Among blacks, it appears to have created a form of displacement. The absence of a notion of class results in the substitution of the notion of race: "upper middle class" became "white."

The complaint that *The Cosby Show* is "too white" is a consequence of this displacement. Although some viewers actually endorsed this criticism, few were able to disentangle the confusion it caused. In the absence of a discourse about social class, respondents found themselves discussing the Huxtables as both black *and* white. One woman, for example, began by praising the show *because* it was black:

> *I really like it. I really do because it shows black people are not like the whites think they are. . . . I'm conscious of them being a black family and proud of them, the way they carry themselves.*

Later, during the same interview, she talked about the Huxtables as sharing the characteristics of a white family:

> *Well, the way they sit down at the table and when they converse with each other. See, I've worked in white homes a long time and I've learned a lot myself by working around them and the way they, their mannerisms really.*

She also pointed to the manner of disciplining the children as characteristic of the upper middle class white homes she had worked in:

> *Well, that's another thing with Cosby, whenever they're having a dispute about or something, and one of the kids would come in, maybe not this one, but "You go upstairs so and so and I'll take care of you later." That's what the mother would say if the kid comes rushing in*

*and they did something. . . . You see, that's what I'm talking about;
she didn't scold her in a harsh way. "Go upstairs and we'll talk about
it later." . . . Deal right with it in a harsh way, you know what I
mean?*

The similarities between the Huxtables and the white families she has
worked for are based upon the commonalities of their class position,
and yet this fact remains elusive. The idea that the Huxtables have adopted
upper middle class cultural norms has been displaced by the notion that
they have become "like white people." Without reference to a relevant
discourse, class differences become racial differences. When this respondent
looks at family, language, and music she sees the Huxtables as clearly
black. When she looks at middle class culture she sees the Huxtables as
white.

A male, middle class respondent revealed a similar confusion of class
and race in a moment of self-consciousness:

*I think the overall concept itself, what's wrong with showing a black
family who has those kind of values? I almost said white values, but
that's not the word I want. There is no monopoly on that kind of thing
that's owned by white folks, but what's wrong with a family living this
way?*

The phrase that he wants is "middle class values," but *middle class* is a
term from a discourse he does not have access to. In its absence he
reverts to the terms of the discourse that he knows and that make at
least some sense: black equals poor, white equals affluent. This respondent's
comments are particularly interesting: he clearly *wants* to break down
the equation between class and race ("there is no monopoly on that kind
of thing"), but finds himself without the terminology with which to do
so.

STEREOTYPING: THE LIMITS
OF CONVENTIONAL THINKING

The Cosby Show, along with most other prime-time television programs,
makes it difficult for people to think in terms of class barriers. This not
only misleads viewers into a benign view of the class system, it distorts
the whole debate about how African Americans should be represented
on television. This failure to deal explicitly with class distinctions has
damaging consequences for the way Americans currently think about the
issue of racial stereotyping in the mass media.

We should begin by noting that the notion of class consciousness was
not entirely absent during our discussions with working and lower middle

class groups. At two moments in the white working class group discussions, respondents expressed a tinge of regret because of the exclusivity of the Huxtables' affluence. These observations were made by two of the poorest respondents in our sample, whose material circumstances were in stark contrast to the comfortable affluence of the Huxtables' brownstone; both respondents used clothes as symbols of material wealth. One woman suggested that, though she liked Clair Huxtable, she would "like to see her more in jeans, or actually doing housework or something," jeans being a symbol of ordinariness that she could relate to. A man in another group made a similar point:

> *The average person watching the show, they're not all that rich. That's something. . . . The kids always have nice clothes on, and I wear dirty jeans because I can't find a clean pair in the morning, whereas if they showed that on* The Cosby Show, *I'd say "I did that," you know.*

Mild as these expressions of class consciousness are, they were, among working class viewers, atypical. Although one or two other working class groups made class conscious statements, they did not do so in response to *The Cosby Show* scripts. The woman quoted above, perhaps significantly, reserved her most scathing comments for the commercials shown during the show:

> *The way they make it look. . . . It really irks me. You know, they never show the family with the mother or father an alcoholic, but they show the fancy clothes, the cars, the wine coolers. . . . I mean, why don't they show the father sitting there passed out in a chair and the kids yelling for something to eat?*

What is interesting about this statement is that it was *not* made in relation to *The Cosby Show*, even though (apart from the mention of wine coolers) *The Cosby Show* is even guiltier of the misrepresentations she criticizes than the commercials shown during it. This suggests that the affluent consumerism of most major TV characters has become so ordinary that viewers no longer notice it.

Only one respondent, a black male, expressed an explicit awareness of class barriers or class structures:

> *I would enjoy it a lot better. . . . I would enjoy it more if they were struggling per se. . . . I mean it seems as though Theo is destined, I mean, you know his father's got a legacy he's going to hand down. I mean he's got everything already. He's got the school planned out for him. You know. No question. It's like white America. It's a silver*

platter syndrome. . . . And I don't think it's like that. . . . I mean I like to see the struggle a little bit because it's not all like that for black America. It's not like that. There's racism. There's the economic situation. I mean it's just not that easy, and I think they make it seem as though "it's here, black America."

Yet even this respondent, in spite of his critical position, finds the prospect of a blue-collar *Cosby Show* a worrying one:

There's part of me that says, in a way, I don't want white America to see us, you know, struggling or whatever.

The problem goes to the root of contemporary thinking about stereotyping. The assumption made by this respondent and by most other respondents in the survey is that *a less affluent image is a negative image*. How pervasive has this assumption become in contemporary American culture?

The notion that the Huxtables' affluence was a positive aspect of the show was articulated time and time again during the group discussions, both by black respondents concerned about negative portrayals of African Americans and white respondents who found the prospect of working class characters less interesting, less admirable, less dignified, or in some cases, downright depressing:

It's fun to watch some classy people do their thing.

People really don't want to see any poverty in . . . This is nice, it looks good and it's kind of, you accept it, they have a beautiful home and everything is okay.

In reference to another, more working class, black show, other respondents commented:

There is still more of the sadness about it. . . . I guess I'm partial to the upper middle class.

But maybe what you love about them too is that nobody wants to see repeats of what they're living. . . . It's totally a fantasy to me, fairy tale, where I think if you bring in the real humdrum of what really life is all about it would be a total bore, tragic smashing bore. The everyday struggle of living, I don't think people really want to see that all the time; they live it too much. They don't want to see that. They say, "Please give me something extra funny and special" and, "Oh, look at their gorgeous sweaters."

I like the fact that they're not a working family; the money just seems to be there. They don't even seem to be working. A working class family, you'd almost draw relations to, they'd have troubles at work, or something like that, so you'd start thinking about something you'd have to do at work. It's almost a separation from that.

It is an attitude that goes to the very heart of *The Cosby Show*. In order to provide positive images of black people, it is seen as necessary to paint them with the golden hue of social success:

Isn't it about time we had a black family on TV and that people, especially little black children maybe who watch it can say, this is a successful family and I will have a successful . . . Well, there are plenty of poor, successful families. I mean, this is a financially successful family and um, but I think, gee, let's give them somebody strong, to kind of, you know . . .

This statement by a working class white woman is particularly interesting. She realizes, just for a moment, the nature of the assumption that she has made: A "strong" or "successful" family means an upper middle class family. Her caveat, even though it makes her conclusion more tentative, nevertheless fails to interrupt the flow of her argument.

As we have suggested, there is nothing natural or inevitable about this common identification of success with social status. It is a sad comment upon our ideological horizons if we cannot disentangle the idea of positive representations of minorities from material success. Nevertheless, the idea that casting black people in upper middle class roles is part of the move away from racial stereotyping is now generally accepted.

Because most black people are far from being upper middle class, the ideological effects of this assumption are deeply counterproductive. The Huxtables and other black TV characters like them are exceptions to the class-bound rules of a generally racially divided society. The rules, which patently disadvantage most African Americans, suddenly are made to appear equitable and just. We are, as a nation, lulled into a false sense of equality and equal opportunity.

THE FICTIONAL CREATION
OF A RACIALLY JUST SOCIETY

To understand racial inequalities in the United States, we need to understand how those inequalities are rooted in a class system. But the representation of class on television (spoken through the language of the American dream) discourages us from thinking in this way. Consequently, the presentation of class and race on television does not help us to perceive racism on the level of class but limits us to perceiving it only at the level of the individual.

Because most white people have little direct conscious experience of racism, the recent proliferation of successful black characters on television would appear to signal a move from a racist to a nonracist society. The success of the Huxtables and other fictional black characters suggests, in the absence of a class analysis, a new era of equal opportunity. The following statements about television, made by various white respondents, were all used to identify what they felt was a new era of opportunity for black people:

> It's like the black family, in the sitcoms in the seventies. It was much more of a working class kind of . . .

> I think they've [the media] gotten better, they're bringing more blacks into different ads, but unobtrusively, so you don't say, "Oh, wow"; you just think automatically, they're included, as they should be.

> But look how far we've come from the days of Archie Bunker, you know, when a black. . . . He was tolerant. . . . But it was a different kind of tolerance; it was almost like he was being a big guy . . . to include them. . . . So now, I think it's good for people to see black families can own nice homes and have careers and have nice clothes and have goals for their children, where for so long, it was never even thought of, considered.

> I think part of it too is that television has become more integrated with black shows.

For most white people, the image of a racially divided world is burdensome because it implicates white people as the undeserving beneficiaries of structural social inequalities. It forces people to confront the need for social change. White people cannot, in the face of such inequality, afford to rest on their laurels without a certain sense of guilt. *The Cosby Show* in this sense is extremely seductive. It provides an image of the world as many would like it to be. Like many forms of seduction, however, it flatters to deceive. It misleads the white audience into the belief that any sense of concern or guilt is unwarranted.

The statistics we presented in the previous chapter make the extent of racial inequality in the United States alarmingly apparent. Television's quiet celebration of effortless black social success, however, presents a contrary picture. We have two worlds: one grounded in social reality, where social injustice is rife; one rooted in television fiction, where social and economic prosperity abound without division or discrimination.

Which world do TV viewers believe in? Most white audience members in our survey, we found, took some of their perceptions of social reality from the happier world of television.

The attitude of most white respondents to affirmative action (in employment, education, and so forth) illustrates such a perception. An affirmative action policy exists as a corrective in a society in which a group of people have been and continue to be systematically disadvantaged. It is a policy that is only equitable or sensible if you acknowledge that society *does* disadvantage certain groups of people. If we live in a world of equal opportunity, however, then such a policy is undoubtedly unfair or unnecessary.

Most white respondents, however, were quite unaware of the existence of widespread or structural racism, and their rejection of policies like affirmative action was a logical consequence of this unawareness. As one white audience member put it:

> *I think that there really is room in the United States for minority people to get ahead, without affirmative action.*

Thus it is with the Huxtables, and thus, in all its old glory, speaks the American dream.

Most other white respondents, in one form or another, echoed this sentiment. Having asserted their own racial tolerance through whole-hearted acceptance of *The Cosby Show*, many were able to proclaim the arrival of an equal society:

> *They should hire the person who knows what they are doing, whether they are black, white, Spanish, or whatever. I don't think they should hire them just because somebody is a certain race.*

> *I don't think every small advertising agency or every small business around needs to have a percentage; if the qualified individual happens to be black, great, but I don't think that it has to be a policy.*

> *I don't think that anybody should be hired just because they are black. . . . I don't think they should have a percentage of blacks, percentages of whites, no, if you're qualified, then you get the job.*

> *I want someone who's really qualified. . . . Don't waste the time and money.*

A Massachusetts Republican and 1991 candidate for Congress, Steven Pierce, when questioned on a TV interview about the lack of evidence to support his claims that gay couples make bad foster parents (WGBH, May 1990) argued that, in the absence of evidence, you should revert to "common sense." As Italian political theorist Antonio Gramsci (1971) noted and as Mr. Pierce so neatly demonstrated, the appeal to common sense is often a convenient way of disguising an oppressive ideology as conventional wisdom. In the discussion of racism and affirmative action, common sense, encouraged by television, leads to the assumption that things are as they should be. As one respondent explained:

> *We haven't lived through . . . I mean . . . I didn't really experience a time where I really saw people firsthandedly treat blacks the way I know they've been treated, you know? I've never seen anybody ask a black to sit in the back of a bus because they are black, and I know that happened; so it's difficult for me to. . . . I can see where they're coming from when they expect, you know, some things because that happened. But I've never seen it, so I don't expect anybody to get any special treatment because of their color.*

Common sense, in this case, was to use limited individual experience to deny the existence of widespread racism and, therefore, the need to do anything to redress it. This anecdotal evidence sometimes involved describing particular instances when an affirmative action policy worked against the interests of what is perceived to be equity and justice:

> *It's misused a lot. I see a couple of guys that I know that lost a job because of affirmative action and they probably were that much more qualified than the minority candidate.*

Often at this point in the interviews respondents would reiterate traditional racist stereotypes, informed by anecdotal images of listless black people languishing on welfare or gliding effortlessly upward on a tide of government assistance and affirmative action programs. One respondent, quoting a black woman she knew, said:

> *"Oh yeah, I got myself pregnant and I'm going to let the state support me for a while." Sure, thanks, let us support you. We're sitting there, busting our butts.*

> *Every job you look at in the paper, it says equal opportunity employer, you know, so you can't say the jobs aren't out there because there's plenty of jobs out there; but they'd rather be on welfare.*

> *We have [black] twenty-three-year-old guys walking in with welfare checks. Why can't they go out and get a job? I'm not getting paid a whole lot, and I'm working. What's wrong with you, you know? I have a very hard time with that because I guess, I think that everyone is,*

everyone should be equal to the point of, if you are qualified for that job then you should be able to get it.

These remarks were made by respondents who, when discussing *The Cosby Show,* were impeccably liberal.

As we have suggested, the effort made by popular cultural forms in the United States to come to terms with racism has often focused on sins of the past, from slavery to the early years of the Civil Rights movement. Most white respondents were, indeed, aware of this history. But white respondents used the acknowledgment of a racist past to demonstrate historical contrast rather than historical continuity. Racism, in other words, is seen by white Cosby watchers as a disease that has been essentially cured; the society requires no further medicine. White respondents repeatedly suggested in this vein that affirmative action is anachronistic, that it belongs to a bygone era of discrimination. This point was made to us time and time again:

Well, I think it has gone too far, where the white people don't have the opportunities. I think it has come to a point where people should be hired now, not because of their color or their race, but because of what they're able to do. I mean there are people who are much better qualified but can't get hired because they are white, and I don't think that's right. Maybe in the beginning, they needed this . . . but it has gone too far.

But I do think it's handed to lots of people that are minorities. . . . We're sitting here, having to pay for our kids and having to pay for our things.

I think I've become less enamored of it. I think that when the whole idea was first discussed, it was a very good idea. . . . In recent years, I don't think it's necessarily getting anybody anywhere . . . and I think that there really is room in the United States for minority people to get ahead, without affirmative action.

I think affirmative action had its place; but at some point it can't go on, it has to stop. I think people in the black community have to understand that. They got a leg up and now they have to go on like the rest of us. Instead, what's happening is, as the standard of living and the economy is going down more and more, and you have to scratch more, push more, and since everyone's standard is going down, it is becoming a bigger morass and they're pushing into . . . Right now affirmative action has fulfilled its need.

I have a hard time with the United Negro College Fund. I think that was great when it started; I think that it had a good purpose then when blacks weren't as acceptable, you know, way back, when they were having . . . I think that it's just as hard for a white kid to go to college nowadays as it is for black kids who were brought up with the same background. If you have the same background and you are brought up the same, the whole life, and they have the college fund for them, but . . .

It's had its place, it's had its time—and obviously something had to be done at some point. I don't like the idea, but they did have to do something; and I suppose that that did work to some extent. But it does get out of hand, and it's got to stop somewhere. I think the black race is being discriminated against in a lot of situations, but as far as getting jobs and things, if they're not qualified for the jobs, we can't be giving jobs to unqualified people. . . . Something they don't deserve.

I think in a lot of respects it's carried too far and that it results in reverse discrimination because you have quotas to meet for different job positions and that kind of stuff; it's like, a white person no longer has equal opportunity toward a job because you have to fill a quota.

And we lose a lot of things; they're getting better insurance for reasons they use because they're black, when in the long run, they're getting ahead of us instead of being equal. And white kids are saying, "If they're getting this, why don't we?" They get all the benefits.

They have an opportunity for education equal to anybody. I would say anyone can get an education if they really want it. I feel that there should be qualifications for jobs.

So they got it easier than the rest of us.

These assessments undoubtedly contradict the actual experience of most black people (as black respondents repeatedly testified); yet they make sense in relation to the world of TV drama, a world where black people, like the Huxtables, have enjoyed considerable success in recent years.

The Cosby Show strikes a deal with its white audience. It asks for an attitude that welcomes a black family onto TV screens in white homes, and in return it provides white viewers pleasure without culpability, with a picture of a comfortable, ordered world in which white people (and the nation as a whole) are absolved of any responsibility for the position of black people.

The Cosby Show is, in this respect, caught in a double bind, compromised by the ideological structures that envelop it. It appears to cultivate both the racial tolerance for which it has been applauded and the profound myopia for which it has been criticized. A more honest message is clearly needed to educate white audiences, yet to include it risks losing most viewers to the safer territories explored on other channels. Racism, it appears, is something that most white viewers simply don't *want* to know about. The world, as *The Cosby Show* demonstrates, is far happier without it.

6

White Responses:
The Emergence of
"Enlightened" Racism

In the previous chapter we suggested that the presence of upper middle class black people on television created the impression among white TV viewers that anyone, regardless of race, color, or creed, could "make it" in the modern United States. We now come to the most disturbing aspect of this misconception.

THE INSIDIOUS RETURN OF RACISM

Although *The Cosby Show* and others like it seem to persuade some white viewers that black doctors and lawyers have become almost commonplace, most white respondents realized that the Huxtables were, in fact, unusual black people. The role of television in this sense is more complicated than it first appears. Our evidence suggests that shows like *The Cosby Show* cultivate, for white viewers, a curious contradiction: the Huxtables' presence on TV finally proves that "anyone can make it"; yet most people know that the vast majority of black people are not like the Huxtables:

> He's not representing what most blacks are. He's not even representing what most whites are—but especially, he's not representing what most blacks are.

> They [the black people the respondent sees every day] are all lower income and have that jive talk, so that I hardly understand them, whereas this . . .

[Father and daughter discussing whether class would make a difference] Money would be a big issue at that point. . . . The house is the biggest part of the show. It's a gorgeous, big house. . . . Do you know how much a house in New York goes for, Dad? You know how many typical black families live in those homes?

Despite their statements about how real, average, or regular the Huxtable family is, most white viewers realized that the Huxtables were not a typical black family. Many observed that they were far less typical than the more working class characters in black sitcoms like *The Jeffersons* or *Good Times*:

It's not a typical black family though. . . . [The] Jeffersons is typical.

[Other black shows] are directed more to blacks. . . . That show [The Jeffersons] tries to grasp as a family, you know, any black family type of thing.

The only show that I've watched on a daily basis was Good Times. *It was so much more realistic than* The Cosby Show. *They were poor, which is easier to make for a black situation considering what the average layman perceives of black people.*

This contradiction, despite some of the liberal ideas that inform it, leads to a decidedly illiberal conclusion. The only way to explain the failure of most black people to achieve what the Huxtables have achieved is to see most black people as intrinsically lazy or stupid. Few white respondents actually articulated such a nakedly racist attitude, preferring to suppress (publicly, at least) the logical outcome of this contradiction. We can see, nevertheless, that the absence of an awareness of the role of class in sustaining racial inequalities means that this racist conclusion is kept simmering (consciously or unconsciously) beneath the surface. Our study would seem to confirm the fears of Henry Louis Gates (1989: 40):

As long as *all* blacks were represented in demeaning or peripheral roles, it was possible to believe that American racism was, as it were, indiscriminate. The social vision of "Cosby," however, reflecting the minuscule integration of blacks into the upper middle class, reassuringly throws the blame for black poverty back onto the impoverished.

The Cosby Show, by demonstrating the opportunity for African Americans to be successful, implicates the majority of black people who have, by the Huxtable criterion, failed.

The show's emphasis on education, for all its good intentions, simply compounds this impression. The Huxtables' children are constantly urged by their parents to recognize the importance of educational achievement and to try hard to get good grades. This provides the viewer with an explanation for the comparative failure of most other black people: if they had only tried harder in school, maybe they would have succeeded. As Bill Cosby says of the Huxtables, "This is an American family—an *American* family—and if you want to live like they do, and you're willing to work, the opportunity is there."

The lesson was not lost on most white respondents. Although they happily welcomed the Huxtables into their homes, careful examination of their discussions made it clear that this welcome would not be extended to all black people. What shows like *The Cosby Show* allow, we discovered, was a new and insidious form of racism. The Huxtables proved that black people can succeed; yet in doing so they also prove the inferiority of black people in general (who have, in comparison with whites, failed).

In his study of television news, Robert Entman makes a similar point. He highlights the contradiction between the black people who appear on the news as stories and the increasing number of black anchors and reporters who tell those stories. He suggests that black people in news stories are mainly linked with crime and special interest politics. Entman (1990: 342–343) writes:

> These images would feed the first two components of modern racism, anti-black affect and resistance to blacks' political demands. On the other hand, the positive dimension of the news, the presence of black anchors and other authority figures, may simultaneously engender an impression that racial discrimination is no longer a problem, bolstering the third component of modern racism, an impression that blacks are not inferior and undesirable, working against *old-fashioned racism* [our emphasis].

In other words, there is a distinction to be made between the crude racism of old and its new, more insidious, and apparently enlightened forms. We shall, in this chapter, explore the origin and character of this duplicitous attitude.

DEFINITIONS OF BLACK: COLOR VERSUS CULTURE

We are used to thinking of racism as an attitude that is crude in its simplicity. The racist discriminates between people purely on the basis of race or color. Although it would be foolish to assume that this kind of prejudice is a thing of the past, we must acknowledge that racism today clothes itself more respectably, allowing a deep-rooted racism to appear to be open-mindedly liberal.

It is easy to forget that race and racial difference involve a great deal more than the categories of physiognomy and skin pigmentation. The differences between a black person and a white person in the United States are deeply rooted in their distinct and separate racial histories, histories encapsulating a host of material and cultural distinctions that render the experience of being black quite different from the experience of being white. Race, in other words, is a social as well as a physical construction.

Racial discrimination, throughout its infamous history, has usually been predicated on a series of perceived symbolic links between skin color and culture. To colonialists, slave owners, and promoters of apartheid, such discrimination meant a straightforward denunciation of black culture as uncivilized, inferior, or threatening. Despite their manifest crudity, these racist attitudes have never been as simple or homogeneous as they sometimes appear. From colonialism onward, the racist discourses within white societies have borne contradictory assumptions about the relation between nature and nurture. Black people have been seen as simultaneously within the reaches of white society and beyond it. The black person's soul was therefore treated, on the one hand, as a changeable commodity open to the influences of missionary zeal and, on the other, as the heart of darkness, inherently irredeemable.

Once placed in the industrial melting pots of the late twentieth century, black people struggling for achievement in an oppressive white world disentangled many of the associations between race and culture. The successes of some black people, against the odds, in a predominantly white environment have made notions of biological determinism decidedly less fashionable. Even limited black success makes white claims to racial superiority difficult to sustain. Although the notion of white racial superiority has certainly not disappeared, it is less common now than ideas of racial equality. But this does not mean the end of racism. Far from it. As an instrument of repression, racism now takes more subtle forms.

In most Western countries, particularly in the United States, the idea that white people and black people are irrevocably tied to discrete cultures has been seriously compromised by the promise of social mobility: the idea that anyone, regardless of race, creed, or class, can change their class. The principle of social mobility is now enshrined within legal structures that, although not guaranteeing racial equality, at least give the idea of equal rights a certain amount of credibility.

Racism is, however, capricious, and it has adapted to this discursive climate by absorbing a number of contradictions. The history of racism, we have demonstrated, is now embedded in an iniquitous capitalist system, where economic rather than racial laws ensure widespread racial segregation and disadvantage. These, in turn, encourage white people, looking around them at the comparative prosperity of whites over blacks, to believe in an imagined cultural superiority and simultaneously to give credence to the idea that we are only what we become.

These beliefs lead to an attitude that separates blackness from the color that defines it. Blackness becomes a cultural notion associated with African Americans, but, from a white perspective, not irredeemably so. It is the same perspective adopted by nineteenth-century missionaries: blackness is seen as a condition from which black people can be liberated.

How is such an apparently archaic attitude sustained in the modern United States? The answer returns us, once again, to the national failure to come to terms with the harsh realities of class barriers. The phenomenon of racism, unlike inequality of wealth and opportunity, is understood not as a consequence of social structures but as the collective sum of individual opinions. If white people as individuals, the thinking goes, stop discriminating against black people, then racial equality is suddenly possible.

We have, we hope, revealed the naïveté of this position. Yet it persists not only among the gullible but throughout mainstream opinion in the United States. Accordingly if, as our study suggests, most white people believe such racism is a thing of the past, then how can we explain the failure of black people, as a group, to achieve parity with white people? In the absence of a class analysis, the answer is to see most black people as culturally inferior. This classless logic says that if most black people fail when there are no individuals discriminating against them, then there must be something wrong with them.

Bill Cosby, whether as himself or as Dr. Heathcliff Huxtable, is easily assimilated into this ideology. He is, as Mark Crispin Miller (1986) argues, visible "proof" of the meritocratic mythology that fuels the American dream, a black person who has achieved success beyond the confines of a racially defined culture. He has, in this sense, escaped from the shackles of his racial origins. It is as if racial disadvantage is something that black people are born with rather than something imposed upon them.

This is racism masquerading as liberalism. White people are willing to accept that black and white people can be equal, and their enjoyment of *The Cosby Show* is testimony to this. They can accept the Huxtables as people who are "just like us." Beneath this progressive attitude, however, lies an implicit and unstated rejection of the majority of black people, who are not like the Huxtables and, by implication, not "like us."

How does this apparently liberal racism manifest itself among the white groups in our audience study? The answer, we shall suggest, reveals a great deal about the ambivalent way many white people *really* feel about black people.

THE BLACK AND WHITE *COSBY SHOW*

One criticism that black people have made of *The Cosby Show* is that the Huxtable family behaves, as Gates has put it, "just like white people." Although this statement is more complex than it sounds at first, it raises an interesting possibility. Perhaps white people do not actually see the Huxtables as a black family at all. Perhaps they see them as white—or as some shade of gray in between.

We discovered that many white people do not view the Huxtables as only black. Just as people were able to see *The Cosby Show* as both realistic and unrealistic, most members of our white audience saw the Huxtable family as simultaneously black *and* white. Before we describe this ambiguous perception in more detail, it is useful to clarify what it means.

Most white people—certainly those who watch *The Cosby Show*—no longer see skin color as a barrier to liking someone or treating them as an equal. Unimpeded by such all-encompassing prejudice, they are able to discriminate between black people, some of whom have succeeded, some of whom have not. However, they quietly (and perhaps unconsciously) retain the association of blackness as an indicator of cultural inferiority, albeit one from which African Americans, if they are talented enough or hard working enough, can escape. This position is arrived at not through malice but through a failure to adequately recognize the disadvantaged position black people occupy in the class structure. This failure is extremely significant because, without such a recognition, there is no nonracist way to resolve the disparity between the Huxtables (and other successful black TV characters) and the majority of comparatively unsuccessful black people. Television, we have suggested, is culpable, albeit unwittingly, at every stage in this process.

This argument explains why many white viewers express considerable ambivalence about issues of race on *The Cosby Show*. The Huxtables are, on the one hand, undeniably black, proving the just nature of the brave, new, nonracist world. They are, on the other, unlike most other black people because they fit neatly into the privileged middle class world of television. Because this world has traditionally been the preserve of white people, the Huxtables' entry into it does indeed make them appear to be "just like white people." It is hardly surprising, in this context, if many of the whites' responses were confused: the Huxtables represent the compromise between black and white culture that is unconsciously seen as a prerequisite of black success.

The degree to which the color was seen to fade from the show varied. Some respondents insisted that, as one person put it, "You can't notice it [the Huxtables' race] at all." This statement is itself revealing. It does not refer to variations in skin tone; rather, it demonstrates the perception of blackness as a function of culture (in its general sense) rather than skin color. Their color is, after all, no more or less noticeable than is that of any other group of African Americans. It is their culture, the way they speak and behave, that makes their color less noticeable.

Respondents were asked whether they felt *The Cosby Show* would be very different if the characters were white rather than black. As we pointed out in Chapter 3, a number of respondents felt that the Huxtables' assimilation into a white televisual world was complete enough to say, as these respondents did:

> *If they were carrying off the thing the same way, you know, really making a satire of life the way they're doing it, average everyday things that happen every day, then I don't think it would be that much different, you know. Because what they do is they really carry it off and say these are the things that can happen to anybody, I don't care if you're white, black, pink, yellow, or green, this happens to everybody in everyday life. That's what they do. They just satirize everything that happens in normal life.*

> *I don't think it would be all that different; they seem to come across . . . I think it is generic enough so that anyone could watch it and appreciate it. Like they acknowledge their own heritage and they happen to be black.*

> *I think at the beginning you would notice it more because it is an all-black show and it was something different. . . . I don't think it makes a difference if they are black or white if it's funny.*

> *You can't [notice color], really! I mean, it wouldn't be any different if they were white.*

> *I would imagine there's some kind of subtlety there that I'm missing, that I'm not picking up on right away. It would have to be different, I would think; but I can't see in what capacity. . . . They don't seem to make any reference to their race.*

This last comment is particularly interesting. The respondent feels sure that there must be some difference, yet she is unable to detect anything identifiably "black" about the Huxtables.

There is an underlying tension beneath these apparently liberal state-ments. The fact that "you just think of them as people," praise for which *The Cosby Show* is singled out, does not prove that race is no longer an issue. Quite the contrary: these particular black people are unusual because they have *transcended* their racial origin and, in so doing, have become normal.

The notion of "average," "everyday," or "generic" that these respon-dents refer to, although it appears to be ethnically neutral, is actually racially specific. The statement that they are "just like any other family" or "just like us" is specific to the Huxtables; it does not refer to black people in general. As one respondent put it:

> *I like the fact that they're black and they present a whole other side of what you tend to think black families are like.*

The Huxtables may be thought to be normal or average, but they are unlike most black families. The everyday world of the Huxtables is the everyday, generic world of white television. One respondent made this point directly:

> *What they're trying to do here is portray a black family in a white family atmosphere.*

Most other group members preferred to make this point by implication, referring to a notion of "normality" that is clearly white. So, for example, when one respondent suggested that, unlike most black TV characters, "they just act like people," he was implying a separation between ordinary people and black people. So, unlike most black people, as another respondent put it:

> *You can just identify with this family, even if they're a different race.*

Similarly, one group member stated:

> *I have Jewish friends, that are so good, that I don't know they're Jewish. . . . There is no constant reminder that this is a black family.*

He was implying that being white Anglo-Saxon is the norm from which others deviate.

These responses are ambiguous rather than color-blind. The respondents knew that they were watching a black family but "forgot" in the face of its familiarity. "You lose track of it," said one woman, "because it's so average." Another respondent described how the Huxtables' race "just sort of drifted" out of her mind while watching. This forgetfulness is simply a way of sustaining two contradictory interpretations of the same thing. The Huxtables are, in this sense, both black and white. This working class white woman, when asked if she was aware of the Huxtables' race, replied:

> *Not at all. But at the same time they don't neglect the black pride which I think is a hard thing to do; and I think they've done it successfully. They've done shows on Martin Luther King and on going down to Washington to do Civil Rights marches when they get together with the grandparents . . . but they do it in a way that's not [too conspicuous or threatening].*

Other respondents replied to the same question in the same way:

> *It depends on what they are talking about. Again, what issue they are dealing with. If they are dealing with something that pertains to black people in particular, I'm aware of it; but if they are not, it really, I don't think it really comes to mind.*

> *Yes and no. You're aware because at points they make you aware, but you could lose track of it because it's so average.*

> *Their attributes are white—in comparison to* Good Times *or something like that. . . . I'd say it's fifty-fifty, sometimes their culture and attitudes, the things they say, bring you back to the fact that this is an entirely black cast, so I'd say 50 percent of the time I notice, 50 percent I don't.*

> *There's something in Clair's voice. There's something in Clair's voice that is not white American.*

NOW YOU SEE IT, NOW YOU DON'T

What makes these ambivalent responses particularly interesting is their particularity to *The Cosby Show*. These respondents were not usually so ambiguous about race. They share a common definition of what blackness is, and they recognize it when they see it. This perception manifested itself when respondents were asked to talk about other, more traditional black TV sitcoms, shows like *Good Times, The Jeffersons, 227,* and *Amen*. While most respondents were able to link these shows under the general category of "black sitcoms," they did not, significantly, include *The Cosby Show* in this category (only one person in the entire white sample made such a link). As one respondent put it, "I think [those shows] are totally different." The difference being that those shows, unlike *The Cosby Show*, involve what is identified as "black humor" in a "black setting."

The black shows that are seen to signify blackness more strongly are, accordingly, compared unfavorably to *The Cosby Show*. These other black sitcoms were often denigrated by white groups for being "slapstick," "loud," "full of yelling and screaming," "stereotypical," and more "black in style and humor":

> *I don't like them, to be honest with you. They're sarcastic, they're loud, they yell, there's no, they just criticize each other openly.*

> *I think they are more stereotypical black shows than* Cosby. *I don't think* Cosby *is stereotypical black. . . . I mean they really don't make much point to the fact that they're black. And certainly don't do black stereotypical things like* Good Times *used to do. But I think* Amen, 227, *are more that way. They talk the slick black accent, and they work on the mannerisms, and I think they make a conscious effort to act that way like they are catering to the black race in that show. Whereas Cosby, you know, definitely doesn't do that. He's upper middle class and he's not black stereotypical. There's a difference in the tone of those shows, completely.*

> *I think there's a lot of black families out there that are similar to the Cosbys that they're not such a stereotype black. You know, talking like the black slang or that kind of stuff, . . . being portrayed as intelligent, white-collar workers and that kind of thing. I should think, from a black perspective,* The Cosby Show *is more complimentary to blacks than some of the other shows. You know, the* 227, *the older woman hanging out of the window watching the neighbors walk by and stuff like that, which is reality in a lot of situations but in terms of. . . . It just seems to be heavy into black stereotyping.*

> Cosby *is much better. . . . The actors are much better, a lot funnier, more stuff you can relate to; they're a lot funnier than the other two. . . . Like* Amen, *the daughter who dates the priest, or whatever he is, you know she's just not realistic, from my point of view anyway. With* 227 *and Jackie, I don't relate to her or care for her at all as an actress, and she's hardly a realistic person. You can get involved in* The Cosby Show *and feel that you understand it, you're a part of it and can relate to it; while on these other shows there's not even usually a whole plot, it's just kind of there.*

> *If you look at* Good Times, *it's a majority of black. It was very racist the going over the white. The "whitey" down the street, you know.*

They [the Huxtables] don't base any humor on black and white kind of thing yet; they let it be known that they are a black family, etc., etc. But the Jeffersons actually made many, many jokes on black-white interaction.

I couldn't picture doing some of those things they did [on Good Times*] or being so desperate for a new refrigerator.*

I don't watch that much TV so I don't watch that many; but I've seen one of them with a black cast and they weren't as funny. Atypical of whatever happens in life and all that.

It's slapstick. It's too noisy for me . . . and I don't remember much about the family, or the interactions, or relationships. Except the slapstick and the volume of it. I'd usually miss half the dialogue. It was all extraneous.

*I remember that it [*The Jeffersons*] was a little bit more slapstick, a little bit more . . . stereotypical. Much more stereotypical. They were more concerned with racial issues, blatant racial issues. There was a couple in the building who were mixed race. And it was much more interested in class, and the difference between class, middle class versus working class. So it was a much different show.*

Running through these statements is a clear dislike of the kind of blackness these other sitcoms represent. The use of the term *stereotypical* by these respondents is interesting in this respect. Normally the term *stereotypical* implies a critical awareness that the stereotype is, in some important way, misleading. This was not necessarily the case with members of our white groups. On the contrary, a vague awareness of media stereotypes was combined with an equally vague assumption that perhaps these stereotypes were, after all, accurate. So, for example, a show that "seems to be heavy into black stereotyping" may also be "reality in a lot of situations." What makes these shows stereotypical for these white viewers is partly that they are seen as unambiguously black. They remind the viewer of racial issues that *The Cosby Show* allows them to forget. So they are "much more stereotypical" partly because "they were more concerned with racial issues, blatant racial issues." These programs are seen as "black humor" for black people; as one respondent says: "Like they are catering to the black race in that show." This perception is not impartial: the blackness on display here is seen by these respondents, almost universally, as negative.

One respondent made an unusual attempt to pursue the question of stereotyping in relation to news coverage, but even she went on to acknowledge that it was difficult for her to make a critical judgment:

You know how they show, in a courtroom, when they accuse someone, and they would probably always be black. And then the white tend to be left out, I think, in terms of crime. And I don't know, is that really what's happening? Or is it just the way the media are reporting it? You have no way of knowing. I have no way of knowing.

In other words, in the absence of other information, we have to accept the stereotypical image as the most plausible one. As a consequence, there was, for the white respondents, only a tiny discursive space between an awareness of TV stereotypes of black people and acceptance of those stereotypes. To condemn other black shows for being stereotypical was, therefore, close to condemning them for being too black. *The Cosby Show,* as a corollary to this, is less stereotypical and therefore less black.

Some white respondents (particularly in the upper middle class groups) expressed their dislike for these stereotypical shows by not watching them at all:

Do you want to know the truth? I tried once, and I couldn't relate to any of it. I don't even know which one I had on. It did not hold my attention at all, and I never turned them back on.

Those who did watch one of these shows appeared to do so without much enthusiasm, particularly when they were compared to the "calm, thought-out" *Cosby Show.* A typical complaint was that they were "less easy to relate to." "They're just not like our family." Just as the absence of race on *The Cosby Show* allows the inclusion of white viewers, the cultural presence of race on other shows serves to alienate the same white viewers. One woman suggested that she was aware of race when watching other black sitcoms, "But you don't think about it with *The Cosby Show....* It doesn't even cross my mind." Or, as another respondent put it, although other black sitcoms exploit identifiably "black humor," with *The Cosby Show* "you just think of them as people."

What do these responses to the Huxtable household signify? In the first instance, it appears that *The Cosby Show* has an appeal among white audiences that other black shows do not. These respondents, as we described in Chapters 2 and 3, had few problems relating to or identifying with the Huxtable family. This identification allows them the enjoyment of taking part vicariously in the pleasant lives of the Huxtables "because," as one respondent observed, *The Cosby Show* "relates mostly to usual, regular families and stuff, and their regular problems, and stuff like that."

Would these viewers enjoy the show as much if its blackness was overtly signified? Moreover, is the absence of any discussion or acknowledgment of racism on *The Cosby Show* a prerequisite for these viewers' enjoyment and participation (as viewers)? The answers to these questions reveal the limits of the apparently liberal perception that the Huxtables are less obviously black because they are, for these white viewers, "just like us." On the whole, these respondents want to be reminded neither that the Huxtables are black nor, still less, of the existence of any form of racism.

A number of respondents were aware, when prompted, that black issues were either introduced with the greatest delicacy or entirely absent from *The Cosby Show*. One respondent suggested that, having been accepted by a wide audience, the Huxtables were able to make gentle references to their race:

> *The early shows, to the best of my recollection, were devoid [of reminders they were black]. They could have been anybody. They didn't have to be black. It was only after the show maintained its popularity for a while that they—I interpret—that they had the ability to keep reminding people that they were black. . . . Suddenly they would be speaking in a black idiom. . . . It's just to put a little bit blacker face on what was until then just happened to be a very good comedy, about realistic people who were played by black people.*

Although a couple of the more self-consciously liberal respondents were critical of the show's failure to go beyond such gentle reminders, most felt that this restraint was positive. Although one respondent did suggest that *The Cosby Show* had now established enough credibility (among white people) to deal with racial issues, she remained unenthusiastic about the prospect:

> *They don't want to deal with the issue of interracial. . . . Life is tough enough anyways, and then to get into interracials. . . . I think if the Cosbys did it, though, I don't think they would have any problems. I think it would be all right, you know; people have a lot of trust in them.*

Most other respondents rejected the idea much more unequivocally. Some expressed this by saying that they watched the show to enjoy it, not to be preached at; others stated that the introduction of black issues would be "alienating" and that the show would "lose a lot" if it dealt with racism, with the ominous consequence that they would "probably lose the white audience they have":

> *I think they'd get a lot of mixed publicity for the show. And it would start to alienate some people.*

I don't think they want to get into those provocative things . . . you know, controversial subjects which raise race, gayness, grievances, losses, yeah, that stuff. I suppose they think there's enough of that anyway. Let's keep this nice and easy.

I think it was intentional on The Cosby Show; *they want them, they don't want them to be a racially oriented show. They want it to be just another family.*

It's the only show I can ever remember where a black family was shown, and they were upper middle class, professional family, having situations that were familiar to most people—well, familiar to that type of person. And race is never an issue.

I think it's low. It would diminish their show. I wouldn't want to see them, you know, doing the black and white thing. Yeah, I don't like that. I really don't think they need to do that.

Other respondents expressed a similar sentiment in relation to Bill Cosby's support for black causes and politicians. Such support made them distinctly uneasy:

But why did Bill Cosby go after this [Tawana Brawley case]? There are plenty of children on the streets of New York that have been raped. And why is he not, as a parent, going after these? . . . Excuse me, but does he also support Jesse Jackson? That really upsets me, about Bill Cosby. . . . So in terms of principles and stuff, I really question Cosby. . . . But then I have to question Bill Cosby's philosophy and principles and everything, if he can stand behind someone like Jesse Jackson. I don't see Bill Cosby in the pure sense that I saw him years ago.

Then you read about him giving money to the Negro College Fund and you wonder, you don't want to watch a show that's against you, you know . . . against the white race.

Bill Cosby is, in these responses, removed from the comfortable sanctity of *The Cosby Show* and placed in a context that emphasizes his blackness. Our respondents reflect here the accuracy of TV producer Norman Lear's assessment of white viewers when he says: "I don't think there's any question that white America is uncomfortable with victimization, or however you want to term the black experience, that which makes you feel guilty, feel uncomfortable" (quoted in Riggs, 1991).

To introduce black issues would transform the Huxtables from a celebrated Everyfamily into a *black* family, an identity these respondents would prefer to avoid. One respondent illustrated this perspective thus:

> *My speculation is that they're trying to present a family who's just*
> *a normal American family. And that, as white people don't talk about*
> *racial issues all the time, or confront them, or deal with them, then*
> *neither would this family. They're trying to get the point across that*
> *it's not an all-consuming issue in their lives.*

To be "normal" here means, as we have seen, to be part of the dominant culture, which is white and, on television, middle or upper middle class. Class is therefore seen as a signifier of race: to be working class and black is seen as being *more* black.

One manifestation of this entangling of perceptions of class and race occurred during a discussion with an upper middle class white group. The group, having complained that the Huxtables, as working professionals, could not possibly cope without some form of domestic help, were asked if such a character should be introduced into the show. Their response was equivocal because, for them, the presence of class differences automatically signaled *racial* tensions:

> *A loaded issue. If they bring in help, what's the color going to be?*
> *Are they going to be treated as a second-class citizen? . . . It would*
> *take some courage because it makes it trickier.*

Questions of class are not seen as generally difficult; they are "tricky" in this case only because the Huxtables are black. The Huxtables' perceived universality is, therefore, partly a function of their privileged class position.

This reaction to class differences is compounded by the nature of contemporary television. The middle class world of television is one without struggle. To admit a black family to this world without disrupting it, the family must, like white TV characters, rise to this social position effortlessly. As far as most viewers in the study were concerned, to include class or racial issues would have made *The Cosby Show* seem less "normal" and ironically, less "realistic."

We can see, in this respect, how television has created a form of doublethink in which it becomes necessary for black characters to deny the realities that distinguish black experience in order to appear credible and realistic.

The general resistance of most white viewers in our study to the possibility of transforming the Huxtables into a blue-collar family suggests that this perception is widespread. The Huxtables, having risen to the comfortable upper middle class world, have, for many white viewers, thereby disentangled themselves from their racial origin. They did not want to see the show, as one respondent put it, "stoop down to another cultural level." To be a blue-collar family, in the media world, would emphasize their "blackness"; as professionals, contrarily, they merge into the "normal" white world of TV. Social mobility, in this sense, becomes a form of sanctity from more unpleasant reminders of racial difference.

BIOLOGY VERSUS CULTURE

The significance of this ambiguity about the Huxtables' race becomes a little clearer when we examine the responses of whites who did *not* articulate it. For these viewers, the Huxtables' race, their blackness, formed a nonnegotiable part of the show. Although such responses were less common among white viewers than some variation of the more color-blind response, they took a number of different tones ranging from progressive to reactionary. These differences originated in quite different attitudes toward black people and race relations.

Viewers who held a number of overtly racist assumptions or were antagonistic in some way toward *all* black people seemed unable to ignore the Huxtables' color. This inability made it difficult for them to identify with the show, and watching it was less enjoyable. Such responses in this study were present only in glimpses. The reactions noted by one interviewer while recruiting participants suggested that some people with strongly held racist views would dislike *The Cosby Show* simply because it was black. One person, refusing to take part in the study, remarked that the show was "stupid, stupid, stupid." Because the respondents were only people who watched *The Cosby Show,* we were less likely to hear this kind of response. Whenever an overtly racist judgment was made, it was fairly blatant. One interview group, for example, was interrupted toward the end of the session by friends, who castigated *The Cosby Show* for being "too black":

> The show is too black. . . . It's too black, centered around the black race.

A more subtle articulation of this reaction came from a viewer who, unlike all the other white interviewees, put *The Cosby Show* in the same category as other black shows. Though he enjoyed some aspects of these shows, he criticized them for excluding white people from their casts. In an inverse version of the discourse of racial stereotyping (used by most black respondents), he argued that the only white people who appeared on the show were "fat and stupid"—this being evidence of what he saw as *The Cosby Show*'s pro-black, anti-white position.

The differences between this kind of reading and the more ambiguous view of *The Cosby Show*'s race is instructive. The more overtly racist viewer is less able to distinguish between blackness as a physical and a cultural category. It is more difficult for those expressing a more overt

form of racism to forget that the Huxtables are black because skin color
is seen to bear an inevitable cultural message. It is a discourse of biological
determinism that can only work to amplify the signifier "black." The
ability of other respondents to disentangle the physical from the cultural
is, by the same token, a prerequisite for their apparently enlightened
failure to identify *The Cosby Show* as a black show.

A few respondents articulated racial awareness in quite a different way.
These people also rejected the idea that the Huxtables could be white
but saw their "blackness" as enjoyable. This idea, though perhaps deeply
felt, was expressed only tentatively. As one woman put it, "It wouldn't
be as funny if it was white. . . . They have a way about them—I don't
know what it is." The inexplicable appeal of the Huxtables' blackness—
the idea that the show would lose an ineffable something if it became
white—was, for some respondents, clearly more difficult to articulate
than the idea that "you forget that they're black." If nothing else, this
tells something about the nature of the dominant white culture, and, in
particular, what that culture allows white people, or makes it easy for
white people, to say about black people. It is easier, in other words, to
celebrate the absence of blackness than its presence.

Only the viewers who were most positive about *The Cosby Show* as a
black show were able to offer any explanation. One referred to her
enjoyment of black culture, while another felt it was more "fun" and
"colorful" because it was a black show ("Black moms are cooler"). These
people tended to be the most progressive in their racial attitudes, and
they usually had considerable experience of black people in their own
lives.

THE CONSEQUENCES OF CLASSLESSNESS

There is a sense in which *The Cosby Show* does appear, for a number
of white viewers, to cultivate a liberal attitude toward black people and
racial equality. The lapses into moments of color-blindness that characterized so many white responses is, in this sense, a major step forward.
The series does, as Dyson suggests, allow white North Americans "to
view black folks as *human beings*." *The Cosby Show* proves that black
people can be just like white people or, as one respondent put it, "that
black people are just like us." The inevitabilities of crude racism have
been disentangled; the color of someone's skin can, indeed, signify nothing.

Before we hurl our hats into the air proclaiming *The Cosby Show* to
be the vision of the racially tolerant society to come, we should reflect
that this victory in race relations is a rather hollow one, achieved at an
extremely high price. For many white respondents, the Huxtables' class
position distinguishes them from other black people, making it possible

for white audiences to disentangle them from preconceived (white) notions of black culture (they're "upper middle class," not "black"). The Huxtables, in this sense, look like most white families on television. If it is necessary for black people to become upper middle class to be spared the prejudice of whites, then it is a price most cannot afford to pay. The acceptance of the Huxtables as an Everyfamily did not dislodge the generally negative associations white viewers have of "black culture," attitudes quickly articulated when other black TV sitcoms were discussed. *The Cosby Show* caters to a need for familiarity, and, in this sense, the price it pays for acceptance is that the Huxtables do appear "just like white people."

For many white respondents in our study, the Huxtables' achievement of the American dream leads them to a world where race no longer matters. This attitude enables white viewers to combine an impeccably liberal attitude toward race with a deep-rooted suspicion of black people.

They are, on the one hand, able to welcome a black family into their homes; they can feel an empathy with them and identify with their problems and experiences. They will, at the same time, distinguish between the Huxtables and most other black people, and their welcome is clearly only extended as far as the Huxtables. If *The Cosby Show* were about a working class family, it would be an unpleasant reminder of the class-based inequalities that support our racially divided society. *The Cosby Show* thus allows white people the luxury of being both liberal and intolerant. They reject bigotry based upon skin color, yet they are wary of most (working class) black people. Color difference is okay, cultural difference is not.

This tells us something about the nature of modern racism. The blackness that many white people fear or regard as inferior is no longer simply a function of skin pigmentation; blackness is seen, instead, as the cultural category that appears to bind most black people to certain class positions, to stunt their capacity for upward mobility. As we have suggested, in a culture that makes it difficult to talk in terms of social and class barriers, this neoracism is the only way to explain why the Huxtables have made it in a United States where most black people have not.

At the same time, *The Cosby Show* panders to the limits of white liberalism, allowing white audiences the sanctimonious pleasure of viewing the world through rose-tinted spectacles. Although we disagree with Shelby Steele's general analysis of race, we concur with his description of the relationship between *The Cosby Show* and white audiences when he says:

the success of this handsome, affluent black family points to the fair-mind-
edness of whites who, out of their essential goodness, changed society so
that black families like the Huxtables could succeed. Whites can watch *The
Cosby Show* and feel complimented on a job well done. . . . On Thursday
nights, Cosby, like a priest, absolves his white viewers, forgives and forgets
the sins of the past (Steele, 1990: 11).

7

Black Responses:
The Hollow Images
of Success

The overriding concern of our black interviewees to discuss *The Cosby Show* in the framework of TV racial stereotyping should alert us to the general function that images play in our lives. Only when controversy erupts, usually about sexual topics, over what should be permissible in the media do most people think about the significance of images. Only then is an invisible process made apparent, forcing us to pay attention to how the images of our environment, to which television is a contributor, affect our behavior and the behavior of others toward us. Although we are presently examining this process in terms of images of blacks, we should not forget that the same issues could be raised in terms of a wider set of familiar images.

THE BAD NEWS

Black respondents first recognized as a problem the relative absence of images of themselves. As Richard Carter says about the response of many black people to Bill Cosby: "We appreciate his show. Since we've got so little, we'd be crazy not to" (quoted in Hartsough, 1989). A female respondent recalled the situation before *The Cosby Show*:

> It's like when I first remember seeing African Americans on TV. "Wow, there's one. Wow, there's one." We're just sitting there saying, "Woop, there's one."

Moreover, the few images of blacks that were available on television were seen as profoundly negative. As we demonstrated in Chapter 4, black invisibility, thanks in part to the success of *The Cosby Show,* is no longer a problem, although the concern about negative images remains.

Almost all black interviewees commented on what they felt to be extremely negative portrayals of black people on television. News programming received the most sustained criticism. Because it continually links blacks with the problems of crime and drugs, TV news was felt to be a prime culprit in the negative stereotyping:

> *I think it's pretty bad. We were talking about that last week, remember. Every time there's a crime, anywhere, it's a black teenager or a black person depicted in the news story.*

> *All the people that take drugs are blacks. . . . It's in a newspaper. I'm certain a lot of white people get locked up, but damn, it's always blacks.*

> *The only people that get arrested are black. And I think they exploit that. They really do. . . . When you see somebody handcuffed, every time you see somebody taking a needle—it's like it's only in the black community. . . . And when they do a drug bust all over this great land. . . . Where did they go? They only go into—on television—into the black community, and they only bust black families. And the only ones that are selling drugs, and the only ones that are on welfare is the black community.*

Notice in this last comment how it is not the police system that picks out black crime, or only blacks who are on welfare in the real world, but television that deliberately distorts.

Discussing the issue of drug abuse, a middle class male respondent pointed out that the problem went beyond merely its production, sale, and consumption, that street activities were merely the most visible part of a vast economy in which white people (who are the predominant property owners in Wilbraham, Westfield, and Longmeadow—affluent sections of Springfield) held controlling positions:

> *It's stereotypes too. . . . If you see poverty and drugs in America on ABC, CBS, nine out of ten times it's on black people, black community. And who controls the drugs? I'd say right here in Springfield, for example, the people who, when the federal government comes in there and the tax people come in to make a bust, they seize homes in Wilbraham, Westfield, Longmeadow. . . . But yet on television, when you see a drug bust, it's always about, you know the Harlems. . . . They never let you see um, you know, who usually does the laundering. . . . White people are doing it. . . . They always show some blacks in negative situations, not too many positive.*

It became clear during our interviews that black respondents were not thinking about these issues for the first time. Such events and issues had already been thought out and discussed with family and friends:

> *I say to my husband sometimes, "My God, don't white girls have babies [out of wedlock] anymore?" Or, "Don't white girls [go] on the dope, and the boys too?" But they don't do that, it's always the black.*

The level of media analysis exhibited in these comments was often quite sophisticated. Many respondents had thought carefully and deeply about the framing of images and their effect on the world. For instance, a black male respondent criticized the way in which television presented black and white women differently in terms of sexuality:

> *Take prostitutes. I was looking at one of those late-night shows on TV. A bunch of call girls . . . all of the white women on there were just impeccably dressed and they may have been Sara Lawrence Grass, but here comes a sister. And did she act colored. . . . Now I don't think that was accidentally. I think that was how TV wanted to portray the sister. . . . The rest of the women there were ladies of the evening, and their sex sales were certainly being put in a different kind of category than the sister's. These people were going to have sex in a fashion that it was going to be acceptable. But the sister was going to some hard screwing. . . . TV does not too often give you a Phylicia Rashad type.*

Clair (Phylicia Rashad) is obviously seen as a much needed corrective to the distorting lens through which television projects the black community.

Another respondent, commenting on the world of commercials, noted that black women were often excluded from the image of beauty as presented by television:

> *The message is, you know, when you see the pretty women, you don't see any black women out there, really. She's white and you know, how many blacks do you see kissing on television? You don't see them that often. Even in a romantic situation in* Cosby, *you know. . . . But I don't see, even with the kids there, they don't get a sustained romance where the. . . . And when you see them in a situation like that, you feel uncomfortable, you know, when they are kissing and hugging on television. . . . I've been brainwashed into thinking that the blacks have certain roles on television.*

Notice the connection between past images, present images, and his own feelings toward them. Conditioned by past images in which blacks have not been allowed the luxury of acting romantic, this viewer is made uncomfortable by *The Cosby Show*'s images of romance and healthy marital sexuality. Past stereotypical images that have denied black people any particular level of humanity act as a filter for understanding new images. This fact accentuates the need to locate the meaning of a television program continually within the broader discourses that limit and control its possible interpretations.

Nowhere among white respondents did we see as deep an understanding of the importance of images in how the world operates. Another black respondent criticized the lack of balance in how black people were portrayed, contrasting their portrayal with how white people were allowed to be human:

> *We seem to be the only people in the world that TV tries to pick out the negative to portray as characteristic of us. I looked at a thing last night called* Appalachia, *a different kind of thing on Appalachia,* 48 Hours *with Dan Rather; and as poor as those people were, and their diction certainly was not up to the level of Harvard and all this kind of business, they were portrayed as very human kind of folks. They don't do that for us. They don't give us that balance. . . . They do that for everybody else but not for us. We can't afford what television is doing for us. . . . But what it's doing to us, I think, is working a hell of a job on us.*

This respondent was able to analyze very perceptively images that did not include him but that he recognized as connected to the way in which blacks could be portrayed ("as very human kind of folks") but were not. He then connected it to a wider set of images (other ways in which white people are represented) that showed the range of that population. He concluded by saying that this lack of range and balance in images of the black population meant that television "is working a hell of a job on us" in terms of how white people understand black people.

Black respondents thus did not look at images of black people simply on their own terms but within a context in which they presume those images to have some effect in the real world. In many interviews, respondents made an explicit connection between negative TV images and the way in which white people come to understand black people. As a middle class male respondent noted:

> *Nobody can believe that you can actually have the intelligence, the fortitude, the dedication and determination to go out and earn a decent living to afford you some nice things. The mentality today is that if you're black and you get something, you either got it through drugs or through prostitution.*

Anthony Walton (1989: 77) has given eloquent expression to the burden that black people must carry as a result of negative images, a consequence of white people treating black people as a group so that one powerful image comes to represent the entire community:

> Willie Horton has taught me the continuing need for a skill W.E.B. DuBois outlined and perfected 100 years ago: living with the veil. I am recognizing my veil of double consciousness, my American self and my black self. I must battle, like all humans, to see myself. I must also battle, because I am black, to see myself as others see me; increasingly my life, literally, depends upon it. I might meet Bernhard Goetz on the subway; my car might break down in Howard Beach; the armed security guard might mistake me for a burglar in the lobby of my building. And they won't see a mild-mannered English major trying to get home. They will see Willie Horton.

RACE AND CLASS IN
BLACK SITUATION COMEDIES

It is now clear, we hope, that a full understanding of the meaning of *The Cosby Show* for its black audience must include their views on the other television programs (including news broadcasts) to which it was often compared—and from which it was seen as an escape and respite. In particular, the meanings generated by the pre-Cosby black situation comedies contextualize the meaning of *The Cosby Show*. We shall now examine the reaction of black respondents to more traditional black sitcoms such as *227, Amen, The Jeffersons,* and *Good Times.*

Those black sitcoms repeatedly came under fierce criticism for their stereotypical portrayals of black life:

> *I've been able to stomach 227 a little bit more now than I was at the beginning. . . . I did not like the stereotypes of the African-American female on the show. I really just didn't. Jackie, you know. At the beginning it was one thing; then the show got raw. They just built her part up to be worse and worse and worse. I mean really until it's getting on my nerves, even her voice.*

> *I've never watched the whole thing [227] . . . that kind of a stout lady on there. Just the little bit I've watched of it, why is it when they portray a black woman in a show, that she has to be full figured and always some wise-ass remarks have to come up? . . . I think sometimes, they try to stereotype blacks on some of those shows, really. And I feel we should get away from that.*

These are comments from people who are acutely aware of the power of images and for whom stereotyping is not just a minor problem, but one that affects their everyday lives. Moreover, these stereotypical representations were seen not simply as one-dimensional but as negative and demeaning. Although other black characters were mentioned as offending in this regard (especially Jackie on *227*) the most sustained criticism was reserved for Sherman Helmsley for his roles in *The Jeffersons* and *Amen*:

> *What I don't like is the deacon as the "jack leg lawyer." Why couldn't he be a good lawyer . . . when they refer to his whims . . . or when he has to do things in a courtroom that includes stripping down to his BVDs . . . I kind of, I don't like that. I mean it's funny, but I don't know that it helps. I don't know that it helps.*

> *I don't like that putting down way he has about him, you know. That stereotype, you know, like, we . . . you know, blacks cracking on each other and sounding on each other and putting down just like* Good Times *and all those shows and a constant put down. I don't like that. . . . People think that's funny. I don't think that's funny.*

> Amen *is funny, but um, it's not following a true-to-life story to me either. I don't care for the deacon. I don't think a deacon would behave that way, and I don't like the way the deacon is acting.*

> *Acting like a fool, making some money.*

We noticed an interesting ambiguity in these respondents' comments. Though a few complained that other black sitcoms were unrealistic, most did not focus their criticism on this aspect. The arguments about realism were saved for *The Cosby Show*. Indeed, a number of viewers thought that characters in other shows were *more* black than the Huxtables but that they were shown negatively in a form of humor that was based upon "putting someone down":

> *That's one thing that bothers me about black shows. Everybody's got to be, you know, cracking on everybody or putting someone down or knifing somebody. . . . You know, like the old shows, the* Good Times *and* Amen *and all those shows. I don't . . . I can't even watch them because it seems like everybody seems to want to put somebody down or all they can say are smart things to another person.*

Other viewers manifested this ambivalence by admitting to a sort of guilty pleasure while watching. Although these shows were being criticized, they were also being viewed regularly (which became clear when viewers started to analyze characters in close detail). People also confessed to finding them funny despite their demeaning portrayals. We found a number of statements of the "they're funny but . . ." variety. A black female middle class viewer reflected on this attraction-repulsion:

> *Oh, [227 and Amen] they're just completely different. . . . It's just plain funny. . . . Now Amen and 227, they have black folk looking like fools most of the time. And its solitude, there in my bedroom, I look at it and crack up laughing. Behind the whole thing and as far as quality is concerned, it just doesn't touch Cosby, you know; totally, utterly ridiculous . . . but they're funny.*

She watches this program, which portrays blacks as "fools," in solitude in her bedroom, so that her laughter cannot be heard. For others this ambivalence was reflected in a sort of act of *loyalty* to black TV shows. A middle class female respondent criticized *227* and *Amen* as "silly" but confessed that she still rather enjoyed them and kept watching to "keep the rating going. I put it on so they'll get their ratings, so they would stay on. They may get better." Similarly, a black female working class respondent commented that she did not "really like that [227] but, again, it is a program that is showing African-American people, family and community, so I support it."

These opinions represent more than a straightforward rejection of stereotypes. Behind the preference for *The Cosby Show* lies a subtle interaction between race and class in the context of an American culture—displayed on television and elsewhere—in which to be working class is a sign of failing in the meritocracy. In the upwardly mobile world of popular television, it is only when black people are presented as middle class that they become normal and are assimilated into the succession of images of social success. The problem with many black sitcoms is, in part, that they are *working class*. Both middle class and working class black respondents interpreted the silliness, the slapstick, the negativity, the put-downs, the stereotypes as indicators of working class life:

> *[What was negative about Good Times] Project, graffiti on the wall, drunks in the elevator, kids sleeping on the couch, you name it. It was just everybody was struggling, the mother was the maid, the father had to travel to find work eventually. I just thought it was like a breakdown of the family. I thought it was negative and demeaning and it does create a general perception that all . . . because white people don't know black people so when they see something like that on television, they, basically in their minds, they think, "Oh, boy"; and then they walk into your home or they just can't wait to get in your home.*

To me . . . [Amen] continues the stereotypes of blacks, you know, and . . . what you call shuffle, and, you know; that girl, she just makes the show, the single girl. . . . The religious, you know, people perceive blacks as religious like going to church and then they go to church and they do all these things, they sing, you know. . . . If I had to compare these with Cosby, he'd be upper class or middle class, whatever you want to call it, you know; they'd be blue-collar type of thing with Helmsley.

227 is more negative than The Cosby Show. *. . . Because the woman in 227 is a housewife, which they [whites] would portray them as, and they are both not working, and live in an apartment.*

*Another reason that I kind of like it [*The Cosby Show*] is because it escapes that whole thing of every black family that you ever saw on TV was poor as a rat's ass. I mean, that is all you got; I mean, "How we ever going to make it? Daddy died and left me with three kids." One of the beauties of it, even that, if it were a crappy show with terrible writing I would still like it for that one redeeming fact. I mean, here were people that didn't fit that J.J. mold and that whole thing because it was such a bogus thing.*

The equation, for these respondents, is quite clear. To be working class on television projects an inherently negative image. Even when the depictions of working class life may be relatively "accurate," they are read negatively simply because they are working class. One could argue, for example, that *Good Times* was a show that attempted to depict black working class life with some accuracy and some degree of sympathy and dignity. Indeed, one respondent read it in that way. But only one. The rest saw the show as fitting the normal stereotypical mode. Similarly one could argue that *Roseanne* is a fairly accurate portrayal of white working class life—far more "real" than the sugar candy world of *The Cosby Show*. Nevertheless, black respondents read it negatively as "slapstick," featuring a bunch of "clowns":

I think it's better to see a professional family because we don't get to see black professional families and that's what makes it to me, give it more of an edge, makes it a little better but you know I would enjoy it. You know, they don't come out like Roseanne.

*I would think if [*The Cosby Show*] was a working class family it would have to be a different situation, because they have—if Cosby seems to talk about education a lot with his children and certain things than maybe someone who was like Roseanne's background, where they seem to be just a bunch of clowns.*

There is, in fact, very little on *Roseanne* that can be correctly described as slapstick. It is a series that, by the standards of other sitcoms on U.S. television, presents an almost gritty realism. Nevertheless, once this connection is made (working class equals slapstick/clowns stereotype), then the only escape is to relive on prime-time programs the essence of the American dream—upward mobility into the middle class.

This logic seems to indicate that NBC executive Brandon Tartikoff's decision not to cast Cliff and Clair as chauffeur and maid (as originally suggested) was, in terms of audience approval, a stroke of genius. To enjoy the ratings success and critical acclaim the show has received from both white and black audiences the Huxtables had to be middle class or upper middle class. Assimilation usually means absorbing and conforming to the norms of the dominant culture. On television, this means being middle or upper middle class. The Huxtables' social status allows them to become part of this world, to be assimilated into television's definition of the normal American family.

POSITIVE IMAGES AND
THE SEARCH FOR PROSPERITY

As we read the comments of black focus groups about stereotyping on *The Cosby Show* and other black sitcoms, it became clear that characters portrayed as working class (let alone poor and struggling) were perceived negatively. As we have seen in Chapter 5, this notion is broadly accepted in our culture by both black and white people, by blue-collar workers and professionals alike. It is, nonetheless, a notion that takes on a greater degree of urgency for black people, who feel (with some justification) that they have been the victims of years of negative stereotyping. *The Cosby Show*, in this context, is much more than entertainment; it is a cultural breakthrough. Whatever their qualms about the show, most black viewers enthuse about it for this reason alone:

> *It's not just a typical—being stereotyped as having only this kind of an interest or going out and partying or you know, loud music or drinking or whatever.*

> *I admire him. I like his show because it depicts black people in a positive way. I think he's good. It's good to see that blacks can be professionals.*

> *That it was a black, clean show and comedy. I like comedy and it wasn't so, it didn't have us acting so stereotype, you know?*

You don't see many African-American role models as them on television. Unfortunately, what we get to see is backstairs at the White House, you know, the maid, the servant; so it is really great to see two intelligent black professionals.

The things that you see on The Cosby Show *you probably will not see on a lot of other places, because they are caught up in old stereotypical white programming.*

There is a great deal at stake here, and most black respondents felt enormous pride in the images of "themselves" that were finally visible to society at large. One mother regarded the series as an important source of nurturing for her children:

When it first came on, it was required watching. The kids knew that. Thursday night was required watching. . . . PBS, Cosby and the news were always free time or anything that we felt that they needed to watch. I mean it was required watching.

Bill Cosby, with his well-known emphasis on the value of education, would find this a glowing testimony indeed.

If only it were that easy. Beneath this celebration of *The Cosby Show* lies a troublesome contradiction. As the reader will observe, Cosby's apparent move to a TV world beyond the confines of stereotyping is dependent upon the Huxtables' lofty class status as "intelligent black professionals." Without that status, the show would be seen as sliding back into the negative territory occupied by more traditional black sitcoms. This status requirement has deeply damaging consequences.

Requiring upper middle class status as a mark of normalcy creates a world that forces black viewers to accept a value system in which they are the inevitable losers. A value system based upon social class (upper equals good, lower equals bad: a notion with a sinister Orwellian ring) devalues most black people, for whom a high-income life-style like the Huxtables' is quite unattainable. Black viewers are thus caught in a trap because the escape route from TV stereotyping comes with a set of ideologically loaded conditions. To look good, to look "positive," means accepting a value system in which upper middle class status is a sign of superiority. This is more than crude materialism; for a group that has been largely excluded from these higher socioeconomic echelons, it is cultural and political suicide.

So powerful is the desire among blacks to escape the negative world of stereotyping that the representation of social reality, the reality of which most of them are a part, becomes a necessary sacrifice. The question of whether the Huxtables are typical or atypical, black or white, real or unreal, is resolved in terms of the broader concerns of the black audience, the desire to overcome TV racial stereotyping. Blacks are willing to accept the unreality because of the broader role played by *The Cosby Show*. They assume that the Huxtables' status is somehow linked to their wholesomeness. A black male middle class respondent, for example, makes the link by constructing a dichotomy between the unreal upper middle class world of the Huxtables and a grisly (and by implication, more "real") alternative:

> *You know, it's always that upper middle class, upper class mentality. . . . It's just not real for me. Again, I like the show per se because it does depict blacks in a more positive way than we usually—we're not killing each other. We're not raping people. You know, we're sane, ordinary people who like the nice things in life like everybody else.*

The Cosby Show may not, in other words, be real; but it is a necessary illusion. There is no space in this dichotomy for depicting blacks "in a more positive way" without elevating them to a world that most black people cannot attain. Other respondents revealed a similar unease with the Huxtables' class status but were willing to accept it because it presented images that the culture accepted as positive:

> *Because to me it puts blacks in, you know, it's a positive thing for blacks, but it's unrealistic; and most blacks, you know. . . . This is a middle class show, but it's appreciated by everybody.*

> *I like Clair's character per se. She's a strong, black woman, very independent. . . . I like her character per se because it depicts blacks in a different mold than what white America thinks. I like the character but again it's TV. It's sort of made up. It just doesn't seem real, but I do like the character.*

The debate about the show's typicality is thus secondary to its power to promote positive images of black life. If the display of wealth is a necessary part of this process, so be it:

> *I've watched talk shows where people made adverse comments about, I mean blacks even made adverse comments, like our children. They say it's not typical. A typical black family. Where you gonna find a lawyer and people dressed like that. . . . It's just a part of life . . . the way things are; but I view this as clean and wholesome. . . . In fact I'd say it's not stereotype, you know, in the negative sort of way that makes it black female, or black male view of downtrod or suppressed.*

Not all black viewers were able to strike this bargain with the series in which a highly selective picture of black experience is accepted because it breaks down stereotypes. Some black respondents found themselves caught in a more self-deceptive logic. Because *The Cosby Show,* as a benevolent intervention in a hitherto hostile world, matters so much to its black viewers, a great deal of emotional energy is invested in it. If this is the show that breaks away from stereotyping, it has to be regarded as real. If it is not real, it is merely another empty image. The tremendous sense of pride in being a part of the Huxtables' world (as African Americans) means that, for some black viewers, any doubts about the reality of the class position of the series have to be suppressed. For it to perform the role assigned to it (showing black people as human and ordinary), the Huxtables have to be reflections of a real world otherwise hidden from public view. As one female respondent put it:

> *I like it because if nothing else, it's giving America a chance to see another side of African-American families that they may not necessarily come into contact with.*

This logic is, on one level, indisputable. If the Huxtables are unrepresentative or unreal, then they are simply another fiction. For if the move beyond traditional stereotyping requires a move into the upper middle class, the pleasure and pride that are experienced in images of yourself that at last you can positively identify with require the existence of a significant and visible black professional class. The credibility of *The Cosby Show*'s move beyond stereotyping is, in this logic, dependent upon demonstrating such a professional class. If it cannot be demonstrated, then the show is only a fiction, just another deceptive image.

THE BATTLE FOR RESPECT

Because black people have made heavy emotional investments in the show on the premise that it realistically depicts black life, a number of viewers, we found, were vehement in their contention that they knew families "just like the Huxtables." This assertion came from viewers regardless of class position. A middle-aged working class man commented:

> *Well, I know there has been a lot of criticism of* Cosby *because people would say that it was not realistic, but it is realistic to have a doctor and lawyer, but the neighborhood that I lived at, may be a little difficult for them to imagine that there are families like this. It's good for me because we are not always showing poverty, despair; we are showing the progress that our race has achieved. That is what makes it real; we have achieved progress. We have black millionaires all over*

> *the place. It is not uncommon to have a black man and a black woman,*
> *both professional making a lot of money, living together. It is not*
> *uncommon these days. But, I think in terms of the media and television*
> *it is uncommon because they choose not to show blacks in this light.*
> *They like to show blacks in terms of crime and in despair, or in negative*
> *situations, and that is why, I think, a lot of people say it is unreal.*
> *It is only because we are not shown in this light.*

The irony of this argument is that, in the 1990s, black prosperity really is quite common in the TV world. In the real world, it is not.

In part, the show is defended so powerfully by black viewers because to deny its reality would also be to deny that black people are just normal, just human. That is, the criticism of the show, especially from white people, is seen as an attack not just on the show but on black people in general. A black male respondent observed:

> *What bothers me about that is this is television. But in real life*
> *people don't want to accept the fact that there is a black family, positive,*
> *black family, intact, in the home, yeah? If Daddy came home drunk*
> *and kicked the butt, that would be all right. If she was big, fat, and*
> *ugly, that would be all right. If the son was in jail, that would be all*
> *right. . . . They disagree and squabble, but they don't knock each other*
> *down and fight, and they don't call each other motherfucker and all*
> *this kind of stuff. The world has to accept the fact that there are black*
> *families, period.*

A female respondent reflected the idea that this "insult to *Cosby* is an insult to us":

> *It's time that the blacks, middle to upper middle class are celebrated*
> *on TV because it's happening now and there are other families like*
> *that. . . . But there are some folks that go to our church that are*
> *white, and I'll never forget when that first came out, she started talking*
> *and she joined the group and talking, and she said "but that's not*
> *real. That's not realistic. There aren't black families like that." And*
> *of course the black people sitting around completely blew up, you know,*
> *but she is not alone.*

The battle over *The Cosby Show* then, is a battle for respect. Once prosperity becomes the basic symbol of human worth, it is necessary to argue that black people are just as likely to achieve prosperity as anyone else. Although some such comments came from the more prosperous focus groups (who were, at least, talking about their own reality), many did not:

I mean for every person who doesn't know that setting, there is an African American who can say "I know somebody who is a doctor" or "I know somebody who's a lawyer" or those professional people. . . . And perhaps it does happen to be where you are living. . . . But in segments of Springfield you'll run into it.

It's just one little show, black people, I think; you know, living decent. It's life; they may not have jokes every few minutes. It may be a little more serious, even in disciplining in one thing or another, but it's. . . . Lots of black people are living now in the upper middle class, or whatever.

Well, let me tell you something, she [Clair] is for real. She's like a lot of sister lawyers that I know.

The whole thing is very for real. And the whites say, "No, that's not for real." A lot of black people are lawyers.

Yet we know there's a lot of black attorneys being lawyers. I know a couple of judges who are women, black, you know, professional wives.

Now I've been in school, and I've heard some kids say that's not real life and putting it down; but there are families like that. It's not a one in a million thing, and there are families like that; and also I think you find people like that.

One respondent took special pleasure in retelling a story of how he took a white business associate to the home of a black upper middle class friend to prove to him that the Huxtables were real:

This white person, looking from white perspectives, and he was amazed and his eyes just couldn't believe there was a black family that lived like this. It was almost like the Cosbys, you know. . . . So when we left . . . it left an impression on him.

The same respondent went to great lengths to point out that the representation of Cliff Huxtable as a black gynecologist was realistic:

And I know a lot of people around the country, black and white, will whisper and say, this is unrealistic. He's a baby specialist, specializing in women and you know, how the feeling is, whites thrown in a black situation like that. But then, in real life, right here in Springfield there's Doctor Jones. . . . He has so many, he's a gynecologist. . . . There are criticisms of the show, but there are some Dr. Huxtables out there.

This firm insistence that there are families like the Huxtables should indicate to us that this is not simply a debate about reality but about identity and respect. Because it is so important, any evidence, no matter how fragmentary or distant, becomes relevant:

> *I'm sure I have, I have heard, I have heard. I mean I heard . . . where the family is a reverend and the daughter is whatever. Then his daughter . . . he is paying for her college. Where I used to work in Westfield this guy was telling me about his girlfriend he knew, and how their family is well off, how they took them to dinner.*

The importance of the reality of families like the Huxtables is indicated in comments about role models:

> *It could serve as, to a certain degree, as role models. It could be a family that youngsters, not only necessarily youngsters but middle class families and not even middle class families can aspire to. To say that you know these kinds of people do exist. And you can have two professionally successful black people doing quite well and the children under control.*

As this respondent suggests, the viability of such role models depends upon their status being attainable. It is difficult to aspire to a status that can never be reached. Another male respondent talked of the need for black heroes, dismissing with some irritation the suggestion that the Huxtables are not real:

> *People start talking about Bill Cosby as not, Huxtable is not for real. Black folks need heroes. Everybody needs heroes.*

CLINGING TO THE AMERICAN DREAM

This insistence upon the legitimacy and authenticity of *The Cosby Show* has its roots in two quite different notions. The first is the widespread feeling that black people have traditionally been stereotyped on television. The second is that human value can, in some way, be measured by status and wealth. In our culture, these two discrete notions have become fused together in a way that locks black people into acceptance of a system that, on the whole, works against them. The ironic consequence of this is that the battle over stereotyping is fought entirely on the turf of the dominant culture, ultimately legitimating white, upper middle class hegemony.

The welding of a critique of stereotyping to a value system based on class, as we have seen, forces many black viewers to argue that the

Huxtables are typical and to suggest that this typicality is proof of racial equality. The problem with this argument is not just that it is wrong (the Huxtables are exceptional, not typical) but that it blinds us to *why* it is wrong. The Huxtables are unusual because the combination of race and class barriers works against most black people. The system is neither fair nor equal, yet many black viewers are seduced, through an argument about stereotyping, into a logic that claims that it is. After all, if the world is like it is on *The Cosby Show,* what is the problem?

To insist upon the existence of a sizable black middle class implies belief in an open meritocracy and, by implication, disbelief in the barriers of race and class. On this dimension we found a curious contradiction among black respondents. In marked contrast to the white respondents, they did not question the need for policies such as affirmative action (their qualms were about its operation and how it has come to be viewed). On this issue, black respondents were reacting to what they knew from their own experience about the problems of equitable employment opportunities. Racially inequitable preferences existed and affected their lives.

Yet many of these same respondents also believed that the black middle class was ubiquitous, that black millionaires were "all over the place." For middle and upper middle class blacks this belief was, not surprisingly, even more common. In comments reported in the previous section, we see the outlines of the broad contours of the American dream. And there were more explicit assertions:

> *I don't believe—I get so tired of hearing "The white man got us down." . . . See, I don't believe that. I think blacks are their own worst enemies. And other minorities come to this country and they make it. . . . I think blacks have just as much opportunity as the whites. I really, I really feel that. I really feel that. We have too many black millionaires. We have too many black successful people in this country to say "Oh, we can't make it." I know too many black people who live—I know just as many black people who live in Longmeadow as I do—as white. And see, I think it's a bunch of crap. . . . I think that my forefathers, my father, they worked hard. And that's how they made it, 'cause it was a work ethic. . . . You know this is bull that we can't make it in this country. It's just bull.*

The notion that it is a matter of "getting our act together" was best expressed by a young working class black male: "I think we just need to pull ourselves together and get ourselves organized like Michael Jackson and Eddie Murphy." And, we would add, like the Huxtables and the other well-to-do black characters who now populate prime time. Although self-help and organization are certainly ways to address the serious problems faced by large numbers of black people in this country, they will not exist or be effective unless the broader structural factors are also addressed.

Unless they address the broader structural factors, the only way that blacks can reconcile real-life economic and social problems with images of success is through individual pathology—blame and self-blame for those who have not made it in the open meritocracy. Because the invisible structures of class, and not the visible structures of race, define the workings of the economic system, the only explanation for massive black poverty must lie in blacks themselves. When this assumption of individual pathology is attached to race, we confront a system of racist belief at the heart of black culture itself, a form of self-hatred.

This is expressed clearly in the work of some of the new black conservatives, such as Shelby Steele (1990: 15). The logic of these arguments is revealing. Steele writes about the decay of inner city Detroit: "Twenty years of decline and demoralization, even as opportunities for blacks to better themselves have increased. By many measures, the majority of blacks—those not yet in the middle class—are further behind whites today than before the victories of the civil rights movement." The assumption here is that new opportunities make it relatively easy to move upward socially. But why has this not taken place? "If conditions have worsened for most of us as racism has receded, then much of the problem *must be of our own making*" (emphasis added).

For all its good intentions, *The Cosby Show* leaves us with an ideological problem. It sustains and promotes the widespread assumption that a positive image of a black person is necessarily of an upper middle class black. This generates contradictory attitudes: first, it "proves" that black people can make it in a predominantly white world, even though most black people have, on this reckoning, failed; second, it cultivates the illusion that economic success is as achievable for black people as for white people. This forces black Americans to buy into a system that handicaps them, without being able to explain (or accept) their persistently low levels of achievement.

The Cosby Show, and others like it, divert attention from the class-based causes of racial inequality. More than this, the series throws a veil of confusion over black people who are trying to comprehend the inequities of modern racism. It derails dissatisfaction with the system and converts it, almost miraculously, into acceptance of its values. In a culture where white people now refuse to acknowledge the existence of unequal opportunities, the political consequences of this acceptance are, for black people, disastrous.

8

Conclusion: Unpopular Messages in an Age of Popularity

"It is not enough to cater to the nation's whims, you must also serve the nation's needs."

—Newton Minnow, FCC Commissioner
to the National Association
of Broadcasters in 1961

The Cosby Show has in many ways changed the way TV producers think about portraying black people. Just as *The Cosby Show* has gone from being innovative to institutional, so African Americans have become a fairly common sight on network television in the United States. And not just any African Americans: many middle and upper middle class black characters now populate our screens. Bill Cosby can be credited with spurring a move toward racial equality on television. Characters on U.S. television were always inclined to be middle or upper middle class; now, in the 1990s, black people have become an equal and everyday part of this upwardly mobile world.

The Cosby Show is, in this connection, more than just another sitcom. It has become a symbol of a new age in popular culture, an age in which black actors no longer have to suffer the indignities of playing a crudely limited array of black stereotypes, an age in which white audiences can accept TV programs with more than just a token black character, an age in which blacks appear increasingly confident of mastering the art of the possible. There is, it seems, much to thank Bill Cosby for.

For these reasons, we began our research genuinely well-disposed toward *The Cosby Show* and the trend it represents. Some criticisms of the show seemed to us a little churlish, chiding the series for not meeting

131

a set of standards that nearly everything on network television fails to meet. For all its flaws, Bill Cosby's series, we were inclined to think, had pushed popular culture ever so gently in a positive direction. Our detailed, qualitative, audience research study has dramatically changed this optimistic view. Our conclusions regarding the show's effects on racism are, as the reader will now be aware, profoundly pessimistic.

We have tried, throughout this book, to stress that the problems generated by *The Cosby Show*'s celebration of black upward mobility cannot all be laid upon Bill Cosby's shoulders. The show is full of good intentions. On one level, it succeeds admirably in promoting an attitude of racial tolerance among white viewers and in generating a feeling of intense pride among black viewers. The fact that these achievements are superficial is not entirely Bill Cosby's fault. The show is caught up in cultural assumptions that go well beyond the responsibility of any one program maker, no matter how influential. What we discovered, in essence, was that the social and cultural context that gives the show its meaning turns its good intentions upside down.

The social success of black TV characters in the wake of *The Cosby Show* does not reflect a trend toward black prosperity in the big, wide world beyond television. On the contrary, the Cosby era has witnessed a comparative decline in the fortunes of most African Americans in the United States. The racial inequities that scarred the United States before the Civil Rights movement can only be rectified by instituting major structural changes in the nation's social, political, and economic life. The White House has, since 1980, withdrawn from any notion of intervention against an iniquitous system, committing itself instead to promoting a freewheeling capitalist economy. This laissez-faire approach has been responsible for the gradual erosion of advances made by black people following the Civil Rights movement. For all the gains made in the fictional world of television, the United States remains a racially divided society.

Maintaining these racial divisions is a class system that keeps most people in their place. The American dream is just that, a fantasy that few can or ever will realize. It is a fantasy sustained by anecdotes and success stories that focus on exceptions, rather than the norm. If we are to begin any kind of serious analysis of racial divisions in the United States, we must acknowledge the existence of the class barriers that confine the majority of black people.

The economic laws of free market capitalism keep these class barriers in place with cavalier efficiency. Our society has declared itself officially nonracist and invited its black citizens to compete alongside everyone else. The game of *Monopoly* is instructive here. If three white people begin a game of Monopoly, a black player who is invited to join them halfway through enters the game with a serious disadvantage. Unless blessed by an unlikely combination of good luck and good sense, the black player is held back by the constant need to pay rent to the other players, forestalling any chance of equal competition for capital accumulation. The United States has treated most of its black citizens in that way. It offers the promise of equal opportunity without providing the means to make use of it. It is the perfect empty promise.

There is a wealth of evidence about the operation of these structural inequalities. What is remarkable about our culture is that it refuses to acknowledge the existence of class structures, let alone understand how they influence racial inequities. And yet, at certain moments, we do accept these things as obvious. We expect rich, white children to do better than poor, black children. We expect it because we know that they will go to better schools, be brought up in more comfortable surroundings, and be offered more opportunities. And our expectations would usually prove to be right. The poor, black children who succeed in spite of these odds are glamorous figures in our culture precisely because they have confounded these expectations. Unfortunately, when we are asked to be analytical, we seem to forget these things. Our culture teaches us to ignore these class structures in a naïve obsession with individual endeavor.

U.S. television fiction is directly culpable for this mass incomprehension. It has helped to create a world that shifts the class boundaries upward so that the definition of what is normal no longer includes the working class. It then behaves as if nothing has happened, and the class barriers that divide working class viewers from upper middle class TV characters simply melt away. It displays the American dream come true, paraded in front of us in sitcoms and drama series night after night. In TV land, everybody, or everybody with an ounce of merit, is making it.

But surely, it's only television, isn't it? Most people realize that the real world is different, don't they? Well, yes and no. Our study suggests that the line between the TV world and the world beyond the screen has, for most people, become exceedingly hazy. We watch at one moment with credulity, at another with disbelief. We mix skepticism with an extraordinary faith in television's capacity to tell us the truth. We know that the Huxtables are not real, yet we continually think about them as if they were. We are seduced by television's fictions to believe partly that this is how the world is but mostly to believe that this is how it could be. We learn to live in the dreams sold by network executives.

Characters like Roseanne, as the viewers in our study repeatedly confirmed, become noticeable because they defy this norm. Simply by being working class, she stands out. The negative response to *thirtysomething* was revealing in this connection. This series dealt, fairly intimately, with the lives of a group of middle and upper middle class people. In sociodemographic terms, these characters were run-of-the-mill for network television. Despite this, the series was endlessly described, often pejoratively, as a "yuppie" drama. Why was this label reserved for *thirtysomething*?

The answer tells us a great deal about the way class is represented on television. The series *thirtysomething* was unusual not because it was about young professionals but because it was *self-consciously* about young professionals. It was difficult to watch *thirtysomething* without being aware that these people were, in class terms, fairly privileged. The series was conspicuously and unapologetically class conscious. When most TV characters display a liberal concern for the poor or the homeless, we are invited to applaud their altruism. When characters on *thirtysomething* did so, we were more likely to cringe with embarrassment at the class contradictions implied by such philanthropic gestures. The main offense of *thirtysomething* was not that it showed us yuppies but that it made them appear privileged, part of an exclusive world that many people will never inhabit. With its coy realism, *thirtysomething* was killjoy television, puncturing the myth of the American dream.

The prosperous, comfortable surroundings in which most TV characters live is much more welcoming, and into this less disconcerting world *The Cosby Show* snugly fits. In order to be normal on television, the show's characters had to be middle or upper middle class. What, after all, could be more routine than a lawyer and a doctor, two of television's favorite types of professionals? It also had to look normal, to portray these wealthy professionals as a regular, everyday family. The show has succeeded in absorbing this contradiction brilliantly. The Huxtables' popularity depends upon this combination of accessibility and affluence. Professionals and blue-collar workers can both watch the show and see themselves reflected in it. Social barriers, like class or race, are absent from this world. They have to be. To acknowledge such barriers would make too many viewers uncomfortable. Television has thereby imposed a set of cultural rules that give us certain expectations about the way the TV world should be.

This makes it very difficult for people schooled in the evasive language of North American television to seriously comprehend the world around them. Any analysis of class structures is simply absent from our popular vocabulary. When respondents tried to make sense of class issues arising in discussions of *The Cosby Show*, many were forced to displace the idea of class onto a set of racial categories. This was particularly the case for black respondents who got enmeshed in the debate about whether the show was "too white." The truth is, the Huxtable family does not belong to a "white" culture but to an upper middle class culture. In the stilted discourse of U.S. television, many respondents found it difficult to make this distinction.

We cannot blame Bill Cosby for playing by the rules of network television. Only by conforming to these cultural limitations was he able to make a black family so widely acceptable—and respected—among the majority of TV viewers (who are white). The consequence of this intervention, however, this "readjustment of the rules" to include black people, is to foster damaging delusions. Television, having confused people about class, becomes incomprehensible about race.

AFFIRMING INACTION IN WHITE VIEWERS

Among white people, the admission of black characters to television's upwardly mobile world gives credence to the idea that racial divisions, whether perpetuated by class barriers or by racism, do not exist. Most white people are extremely receptive to such a message. Like Ronald Reagan's folksy feelgood patriotism, the idea allows them to feel good about themselves and about the society they are part of. The Cosby-Huxtable persona (along with the many other black professionals it has brought forth in the TV world) tells viewers that, as one respondent put it, "there really is room in the United States for minorities to get ahead, without affirmative action."

The whole notion of affirmative action has become a hot issue in contemporary politics. Republicans (with a few exceptions) use their opposition to it, as Jesse Helms showed during his 1990 senatorial campaign, as a way of mobilizing white voters. Our study is good news for these Republicans. It reveals that the opposition to affirmative action among white respondents was overwhelming. What was particularly notable was that although most white people are prepared to acknowledge that such a policy was once necessary, the prevailing feeling was that this was no longer so. (As our discussion in Chapter 4 showed, the positive effects of the affirmative action policy have been confined almost exclusively to middle class blacks, a fact that no one in our sample discussed. The assumption was that affirmative action is something that *all* black people have benefited from.)

There are, of course, circumstances in which a well-qualified black person will receive a warm reception from employers concerned to acquire an "equal opportunity" image. Any cursory glance at social statistics, however, will show that this is because employers are embarrassed by current levels of inequality in the workplace. Almost any social index will show that we live in a society in which black and white people as groups are not equal—not in education, health, housing, employment, or wealth. So why is affirmative action suddenly thought to be no longer necessary? Partly, we would suggest, because our popular culture tells us so.

During our analysis of the content of three major networks' programming, we came across only one program, *Quantum Leap*, that offered a glimpse of these racial divisions. What was significant about this program, however, was that the story took place not in the present but in the past, during the early days of the Civil Rights movement. *Quantum Leap* was only able to show us racial divisions in the United States by traveling back in time to the "bad old days." All black characters in stories set in the present seemed blissfully free of racial impediments. Recent attempts by Hollywood to deal with racial inequality adopt the same strategy. Racism, whether in *Mississippi Burning, Driving Miss Daisy,* or *The Long Walk Home,* is safely confined to history. There are, of course, some exceptions (notably the work of Spike Lee), but the general impression is clear: racial inequality is behind us; we now live in Bill Cosby's brave new world, where anyone can make it.

Television, despite the liberal intentions of many of its writers, has pushed our culture backward. White people are not prepared to deal with the problem of racial inequality because they no longer see that there *is* a problem. *The Cosby Show,* our study showed, is an integral part of this process of public disenlightenment. Commercial television becomes Dr. Feelgood, indulging its white viewers so that their response to racial inequality becomes a guilt-free, self-righteous inactivity. Television performs an ideological conjuring trick that plays neatly into the hands of free market proponents in the Republican party, with their irresistible recipe of "don't worry, be happy."

This retrograde development has burdened us with a new, repressed form of racism. Although television portrays a world of equal opportunity, most white people know that in the world at large, black people achieve less material success, on the whole, than white people. They know that black people are disproportionately likely to live in poor neighborhoods and drop out of school. How can this knowledge be reconciled with the smiling faces of the Huxtables? If we are blind to the roots of racial inequality embedded in our society's class structure, then there *is* only one way to reconcile this paradoxical state of affairs. If white people are disproportionately successful, then they must be disproportionately smarter or more willing to work hard. The face of Cliff Huxtable begins to fade into the more sinister and threatening face of Willie Horton. Although few respondents were prepared to be this explicit (although a number came close), their failure to acknowledge class or racial barriers means that this is the only other explanation that makes any sense.

This explanation for black poverty underlies the increasingly influential analysis of urban poverty put forward by conservative policymakers.

Commenting on this, William Julius Wilson in *The Truly Disadvantaged* (1987) argues that whereas a few years ago liberal perspectives (based upon highlighting racial discrimination and social class oppression) were most influential in shaping how the government thought about dealing with urban poverty, conservative spokespeople are most listened to now. The main thrust of the conservatives' analysis is that the problems of the ghetto underclass originate from the culture of that class itself and that the solution is to change their values. If the underclass members do not succeed, in other words, then it is all their own fault.

The culture of poverty thesis has been lurking in the wings for over a hundred years. The growth of social science in the twentieth century has led to a dismissal of such an intellectually feeble and sociologically naïve notion as quaint—something we used to believe before we knew any better. To see such a reactionary notion become fashionable once again would be ludicrous if it were not so serious. As we approach the twenty-first century, we seem content to abandon all we have learned since the early days of social reform only to embrace an idea that allows our political leaders to pay tribute to a sprinkling of missionaries (a thousand points of light) while abandoning social reform altogether.

Television is partly responsible for this lurch backward. The Huxtables are examples of blacks who have changed their culture and thus their socioeconomic status. Without being able to see the Huxtables and the black ghetto underclass separated by class, television (and the rest of popular culture) stresses instead their unity. If there are families like the Huxtables (which, of course, there are), then the inadequacies of ghetto underclass members themselves explain their social position. That more blacks are in this disadvantaged position than whites further indicates a racial pathology in which the culture of black people keeps them in their place. Sociologist Herman Gray (in Riggs, 1991) comments that *The Cosby Show* plays a role in mediating the polarization between rich and poor that characterized the 1980s: "We come away with the sense in which the society is fine, there's no problem, you just have to work hard, you just have to have the right kind of values, have the right kind of desires and aspirations, and it'll be alright."

Wilson is concerned to put forward policies that will be not only effective but able to capture the support and imagination of the general population. Our evidence suggests that liberal policies focused on the historical effects of racism and the contemporary effects of economic deprivation will now be very difficult to sell.

What we end up with, in the apparently enlightened welcome that white viewers extend to the Huxtables, is a new, sophisticated form of racism. The Huxtables' success implies the failure of a majority of black people who, by these standards, have not achieved similar professional or material success. Television, which tells us nothing about the structures behind success or failure, leaves white viewers to assume that black people who do not measure up to their television counterparts have only themselves to blame. In this regard, notes cultural critic Patricia Turner, *The Cosby Show* "is very appealing to white audiences because it reinforces the notion that the Civil Rights movement took care of all the racial inequalities in the society" (in Riggs, 1991).

RETHINKING STEREOTYPES

In a rather different way, the effect of *The Cosby Show* on its black audience is also one of flattering to deceive. The dominant reaction of black respondents to the series was "for this relief much thanks." After suffering years of negative media stereotyping, most black viewers were delighted by a show that portrayed African Americans as intelligent, sensitive, and *successful*.

The problem with this response is that it accepts the assumption that, on television, a positive image is a prosperous image. This dubious equation means that African Americans are trapped in a position where any reflection of a more typical black experience—which is certainly *not* upper middle class—is "stereotypical." As one black respondent said, even though he was aware that *The Cosby Show* presented a misleading picture of what life was like for most black Americans, "There's part of me that says, in a way, I don't want white America to see us, you know, struggling or whatever." Among white Americans, the feeling, as we have seen, is mutual.

This analysis of stereotyping of black people dominates contemporary thought. It is the consequence of a TV world that has told us that to be working class is to be marginal. To be normal on network television in the United States, our popular culture tells us, you have to be middle or upper middle class. Viewers are therefore able to see the Huxtable family as both regular, average, and everyday *and* as successful, well-heeled professionals. This may be Orwellian doublethink, and it is encouraged by television.

For black viewers, this duplicity amounts to a form of cultural blackmail. It leaves them two choices. Either they are complicit partners in an image system that masks deep racial divisions in the United States, or they are forced to buy into the fiction that "there are black millionaires all over the place," thereby accepting *The Cosby Show* as a legitimate portrayal of ordinary African-American life. After years of resentment at television's portrayal of black people, to end up with such a choice is a cruel injustice to most black people.

As we have suggested, it doesn't have to be this way. There is no reason why TV characters cannot be working class and dignified, admirable, or even just plain normal. Other TV cultures have managed to avoid distorting and suppressing the class structure of their societies; why can't we manage it in the United States? There are, we suggest, two main obstacles, the first ideological, the second economic.

MOVING BEYOND THE AMERICAN DREAM

It is now about four decades since Arthur Miller wrote *Death of a Salesman*. The Pulitzer prizewinning play tells the story of an ordinary middle class family trapped within the aspirations of the American dream, a story that becomes tragic as the gap between the family's actual life and the dream becomes increasingly evident. The play's frustrated protagonist, Willy Loman, becoming desperate with the ordinariness of his own life, finally loses his grip on reality altogether. It is a sobering lesson that the United States has failed utterly to learn.

The American dream is much more than a gentle fantasy; it is a cultural doctrine that encompasses vast tracts of American life. No politician would dare to question our belief in it any more than they would publicly question the existence of God. Even though politicians of many different persuasions pay lip service to the dream (it is, in conventional wisdom, "what's great about America"), it is no longer a politically neutral idea. It favors persons on the political right who say that anyone, regardless of circumstance or background, can make it if they try. In such an egalitarian world, the free market can reign unrestrained. For government to intervene to eradicate the enormous social problems in the United States would be to defy the logic of the dream. Intervention would imply, after all, that the world is not naturally fair and that opportunity is not universal.

The American dream is insidious, not innocent. It is part of a belief system that allows people in the United States to disregard the inequities that generate the nation's appalling record (by comparison with almost any other industrially developed nation) on poverty, crime, health, homelessness, and education. It is to be expected, perhaps, that more fortunate persons cling to the self-justifying individualism that the dream promotes. One of the strangest things about the United States is that less fortunate persons do so too.

The ideological dominance of the American dream is sustained by its massive presence in popular culture. The TV and film industries churn out fable after fable, reducing us to spellbound passivity. The success we are encouraged to strive for is always linked to the acquisition of goods. This whole materialistic charade is fueled by the most influential cultural industry in the United States: advertising.

Advertising is everywhere in the United States. Billboards loom over us whether we're in the city or the country, and posters and handbills decorate nearly every public place. Shopping areas from downtown districts to suburban malls to the ubiquitous small-town strip are littered with logos and commercial messages. Television, radio, newspapers, and magazines are saturated with advertising. It clutters our mailboxes and even our clothing. With commercial slogans emblazoned across baseball caps, T-shirts and sneakers, we become walking advertisements.

Though such artifacts are not unique to the United States, this nation carries advertising to an unmatched excess. And what do these advertising messages say to us? Consume; then aspire to a level where we can consume more. Our contentment is anathema to the advertising industry: We have to be encouraged to be in a state of constant material desire. The economic logic of the industry requires that we never be happy. We can exist only on the verge of happiness, always at least one more consumer item away from contentment.

The key word in this acquisitive lexicon is *aspiration*. Consumers do not usually see themselves in commercials; they see a vision of a glamorous and affluent world they aspire to be part of. Underlying the preponderance of middle and upper middle class characters on display is the relentless message that the world of happiness and contentment looks like their world. It is not surprising, then, that we assume that more ordinary settings are necessarily gloomy or depressing. As a middle class white woman in our study put it, "Nobody wants to see repeats of what they're living. . . . The everyday struggle of living, I don't think people really want to see all that . . . they say, 'please give me something extra funny and special,' and 'Oh, look at those gorgeous sweaters.'" In other words, we expect television to be more dramatic than everyday life, and, in the United States, we also expect it to be more affluent. We don't just want a good story, we want a "classy" setting. This is the language of advertising. It is now also the discourse of the American dream. This language is now so important in our culture that these attitudes seem perfectly natural. Only when we look at other TV cultures can we see that they are not.

This discourse of aspiration permeates our popular culture. Few other industrial nations allow their cultural industries to be as dependent upon advertising revenue as does the United States. Little happens in the popular culture of the United States without a commercial sponsor. In this lightly regulated free market economy, cultural industries are not accountable to a notion of public service, only to the bottom line of profitability. Unlike most other Western governments, the United States spends little public money on art and culture. In 1990, the government spent only $171 million on the National Endowment for the Arts, less than it allocated to the Pentagon for military bands. This amounts to around 70 cents per capita spent on art and culture. In West Germany the per capita figure, over $70, is a hundred times greater. Even the British, after more than a decade of free market government policy, spent nearly twenty times as much per capita.

Apart from minuscule grants to public broadcasting, the survival of radio and TV stations depends almost entirely on their ability to sell consumers (listeners or viewers) to advertisers. Moreover, broadcasters in the United States are required to do little in the way of public service. No regulations encourage quality, diversity, innovation, or educational value in programming. This means that the influence of advertising is twofold. Not only does it create a cultural climate that influences the form and style of programs that fill the spaces between commercials; it also commits television to the production of formulaic programming. Once television establishes cultural patterns, it is reluctant to deviate from them for fear of losing the ratings that bring in the station's revenue.

In this regard it is instructive to look at a couple of series that deviated from the norms that we have examined in this book. The first is the 1970s show *Good Times* (developed by TV producer Norman Lear), set in the housing projects of Chicago's South Side. Henry Louis Gates, speaking in producer/director/writer Marlon Riggs's superb 1991 film *Color Adjustment,* refers to the show as reflecting both:

> the greatest potential and, in my opinion, the greatest failure. Greatest potential because it was an inner-city family that was nuclear and solid. They would talk about real-world issues, and how an actual black family deals with those real-world issues of racism and economic discrimination. But what happened? They elevated J.J.'s role, which had been one of amusing and sometimes sophisticated comedy, to that of a buffoon.

Audience research found that viewers responded well to comedian Jimmy Walker's character, J.J., and driven by the logic of ratings he took on a new prominence in the show, diverting and ultimately eclipsing the other issues the show dealt with. By turning him into a (black) minstrel, traditional audience prejudices could be used for greatest advantage. As Norman Lear now comments on this: "The audience just loved it, but we erred by giving them too much and not stopping sooner."

The other series that has presented a profoundly different African-American face on television is the 1980s series *Frank's Place,* produced by and starring actor Tim Reid. Again Henry Louis Gates (in Riggs, 1991) comments on this: "For many people *Frank's Place* was the best television program involving black people that there's ever been. *Frank's Place* showed a broader range of types than any other black television program that I can remember, but it was killed by the ratings." Tim Reid reports a constant tension between the show's writers and the network, with the latter trying to fit the show into the traditional confines of black situation comedy. "We looked for the unusual but we caught constant flak [from the network]. They didn't want us to do it. They kept wanting us to be funny. If we had been funnier we'd most probably still be on the air. They really want you to be colorless. They want you not to bring your race with you."

The reasons for the dismissal of the series from the prime-time schedule tell us much about the workings and expectations of commercial television. Gates (in Riggs, 1991) argues: "*Frank's Place* was too real for Americans. It was the closest thing to the reality I experienced growing up and the reality I experience now as a person of color in American society that I have ever encountered on television, and I don't think that the average white American is prepared to encounter the full complexity of that reality. They want to encounter fictions of that reality which are palatable to them."

As we have shown, the range of acceptable black American depictions is severely constrained by the workings and logic of commercial television and the perceived needs of the mass (largely white) audience. Tim Reid (in Riggs, 1991) comments that white audiences were "very uncomfortable with *Frank's Place*. And I understand that and I'm not saying that's the worst thing in the world. It's just that I'm comfortable with my people, I'm comfortable with my background, I want to see my story told." But it is a story that has integrity for only a minority of television viewers and is a cultural threat for the majority. Although from the perspective of "public service" the need to present such a story could be defended from attack, in a system that recognizes only volume and profit margins, it is a story confined to the dreams of black writers and artists.

Which brings us back to *The Cosby Show*. In order to be successful and to stay on the air, *The Cosby Show* had to meet certain viewer expectations. This, as we have seen, meant seducing viewers with the vision of comfortable affluence that the Huxtables epitomize. Once television has succumbed to the discourse of the American dream, in which a positive image is a prosperous one, it cannot afford the drop in ratings that would likely accompany a redefinition of viewers' expectations. TV series that depart from conventional viewer expectations are necessarily short-lived. Series like *Frank's Place, Cop Rock, Twin Peaks,* or even *thirtysomething* all deviated from a norm; and, though watched by millions of viewers, they did not attain the mass audience required to keep them on the air. This puts us on a treadmill of cultural stagnation.

Mainstream taste cannot significantly change or develop because it is rarely allowed to change or develop. Innovation, in a system that requires an immediate return on investment, is too great an economic risk. In such a system, it pays to meet viewers' expectations rather than upset them; the bland repetition of feelgood fantasies makes sound business sense. There are exceptions, of course, but they are infrequent. It could be argued that the only genuinely innovative show that has survived in the commercial sector of this cultural quagmire in recent years is *The Simpsons*.

In such a system, *The Cosby Show*'s survival depends upon meeting the demands of a formula that pleases as many people as possible. The series meets those demands with consummate success, pleasing blacks and whites, blue-collar workers and professionals, all in slightly different ways. It plays with an ambiguity that maximizes its audience. For *The Cosby Show* to challenge viewers' associations built up over the years of television that have preceded it, it would have to confront the culturally pervasive discourse of the American dream. This, in turn, would mean rethinking the way television is funded and regulated in the United States. The societal problems we have identified in the post-Cosby era, in other words, go far beyond the harmonious world inside the Huxtables' New York brownstone.

What we are suggesting is that we reconsider the whole notion of media stereotyping by examining the ideological and economic conditions that underpin it. If we do not, we place our culture on a never-ending treadmill of images and attitudes without ever giving ourselves, as a society, the time to think about the consequences of those images. Discussions about television's influence tend to be limited to the effect of its use of sex or violence. If our audience response study tells us anything, it is that we need to be more attentive to the attitudes cultivated by normal, everyday television. In the case of *The Cosby Show*, these attitudes can affect the way we think about issues like race and class and, in so doing, even influence the results of elections.

Herman Gray (in Riggs, 1991) addresses this issue, and possible solutions to the problems we have outlined, when he says:

> What we get is a continuing press towards an imaginary middle . . . whether it's a class middle, whether it's a racial norm, whether it's some ideological aspiration of what the good life is. I think what we need are more complicated ways of imagining ourselves in the world, that are truer to what people know and what people's imaginations are about. And that those things are inflected by difference, and that what we need to do is begin to illuminate that difference, not so that people are divided and can't have access to each other, but so that one understands the ways in which inequality gets perpetrated

and operates. But also so that we learn more about each other and more about ourselves. And I think that television simply hasn't done that.

This is a call for diversity and variety and goes to the heart of how a democratic society works.

Our culture is much too important to be left to the lowest common denominator laws of the free market. We must begin to think qualitatively as well as quantitatively: choice should mean lots of different programs, not lots of different channels. Something is rotten in the state of television, and we should do something about it.

It is often said that a key characteristic of societies that claim to be democratic is their toleration and even support for messages that are not popular. The well-known argument goes something like this: "I totally disagree with what you say, but I will defend to the death your right to say it." A noble sentiment, it recognizes that democratic societies remain healthy and prosperous by encouraging debate and diversity. Yet in the United States we have permitted the television industry to be controlled by the notion of "popularity," which is what determines profitability. In the quest for large numbers of viewers, program makers cannot afford to confront viewers with challenging or unpopular messages. Lost viewers translate into loss of advertising revenue and ultimately to a show's cancellation.

For many reasons, which we have examined in this book, Americans, whether black or white, do not want to see working class black people play a part in television's stories or to see those stories deal with problems of crime, poverty, joblessness, broken families, or drug addiction. The only black people they will invite into their homes regularly are people like the Huxtables. Program makers are not interested in the public good but in their private investment: if enough of the audience does not want something, then no part of the audience gets it. In such a context the prejudices of the audience have to be played to. To challenge and try to change those prejudices would result in financial failure within the present arrangements of American commercial television.

We suggest that what is needed is a television system that will air unpopular messages and, in part, honestly confront the central problems of the day. If Bill Cosby can make large numbers of white Americans identify with a black middle class family, perhaps someone else could do the same for a black working class family if they were granted *the time*. The challenge for the people who control network television is to find the integrity and courage to allow socially unpopular or unconventional messages a presence in spite of the risks. Without such a commitment, television discourse will have more in common with authoritarianism than with democracy. We must admit to not being hopeful about the prospects.

References

Aronowitz, Stanley. 1989. "Working Class Culture in an Electronic Age." In *Cultural Politics in Contemporary America,* edited by I. Angus and S. Jhally. New York: Routledge.

Bourdieu, Pierre. 1984. *Distinction.* Cambridge, Mass.: Harvard University Press.

Bowles, Sam. 1986. "Schooling and Inequality." In *The Capitalist System,* edited by R. Edwards, M. Reich, and T. Weisskopf. Englewood-Cliffs, NJ: Prentice-Hall.

Center for Popular Economics. 1986. *Economic Report of the People.* Boston: South End Press.

DeMott, Benjamin. 1990. *The Imperial Middle: Why Americans Can't Think Straight About Class.* New York: William Morrow and Co.

Downing, John. 1988. *"The Cosby Show* and American Racial Discourse." In *Discourse and Discrimination,* edited by Geneva Smitherman-Donaldson and T. van Dijk. Michigan: Wayne State University Press.

Dyson, Michael. 1989. "Bill Cosby and the Politics of Race." *Zeta,* September.

Entman, Robert. 1990. "Modern Racism and the Images of Blacks in Local Television News." *Critical Studies in Mass Communication* 7 (no. 4, December).

Gates, Henry Louis. 1989. "TV's Black World Turns—But Stays Unreal." *New York Times,* November 12.

Gramsci, Antonio. 1971. *Selections from the Prison Notebooks.* London: Lawrence and Wishart.

Hartsough, Denise. 1989. *"The Cosby Show* in Historical Context: Explaining its Appeal to Middle-Class Black Women." Paper presented to the Ohio University Film Conference.

Katz, Elihu and Tamar Liebes. 1985. "Mutual Aid in the Decoding of *Dallas.*" In *Television in Transition,* edited by P. Drummond and R. Paterson. London: British Film Institute.

Lewis, Justin. 1991. *The Ideological Octopus: An Exploration of Television and Its Audience.* New York: Routledge.

Miller, Mark Crispin. 1986. "Deride and Conquer." In *Watching Television: A Pantheon Guide to Popular Culture,* edited by Todd Gitlin. New York: Pantheon.

Morgan, Michael. 1989. "Television and Democracy." In *Cultural Politics in Contemporary America,* edited by I. Angus and S. Jhally. New York: Routledge.

Morley, David. 1986. *Family Television.* London: Comedia.

Press, Andrea. 1991. *Women Watching Television.* Philadelphia: University of Pennsylvania Press. (Page numbers in text are to draft manuscript.)

Real, Michael. 1991. "Bill Cosby and Recoding Ethnicity." In *Television Criticism,* edited by Leah R. Vande Berg and L. A. Wenner. New York: Longman.

Reed, Ishmael. 1991. "Tuning out Network Bias." *New York Times,* OP-ED, Tuesday, April 9.

Riggs, Marlon. 1991. *Color Adjustment* (a film produced, directed, and written by Marlon Riggs). San Francisco, Calif.: California Newsreel

Rosen, Ruth. 1986. "Soap Operas: Search for Yesterday." In *Watching Television: A Pantheon Guide to Popular Culture,* edited by Todd Gitlin. New York: Pantheon.

Steele, Shelby. 1990. *The Content of Our Character.* New York: Harper Perennial.

United States Department of Commerce. 1991. *Statistical Abstract of the United States, 1990.* Washington, D.C.: U.S. Government Printing Office.

Walton, Anthony. 1989. "Willie Horton and Me." *The New York Times Magazine,* August 20.

Williams, Raymond. 1961. *The Long Revolution.* New York: Columbia University Press.

Wilson, W. J. 1980. *The Declining Significance of Race.* 2d ed. Chicago: University of Chicago Press.

———. 1987. *The Truly Disadvantaged.* Chicago: University of Chicago Press.

About the Book & Authors

The Cosby Show needs little introduction to most people familiar with American popular culture. It is a show with immense and universal appeal. Even so, most debates about the significance of the program have failed to take into account one of the more important elements of its success—its viewers. Through a major study of the audiences of *The Cosby Show,* the authors treat two issues of great social and political importance—how television, America's most widespread cultural form, influences the way we think, and how our society in the post–Civil Rights era thinks about race, our most widespread cultural problem.

This book offers a radical challenge to the conventional wisdom concerning racial stereotyping in the United States and demonstrates how apparently progressive programs like *The Cosby Show,* despite good intentions, actually help to construct "enlightened" forms of racism. The authors argue that, in the post–Civil Rights era, a new structure of racial beliefs, based on subtle contradictions between attitudes toward race and class, has brought in its wake this new form of racial thought that seems on the surface to exhibit a new tolerance. However, professors Jhally and Lewis find that because Americans cannot think clearly about class, they cannot, after all, think clearly about race.

This groundbreaking book is rooted in an empirical analysis of the reactions to *The Cosby Show* of a range of ordinary Americans, both black and white. Professors Jhally and Lewis discussed with the different audiences their attitudes toward the program and more generally their understanding and perceptions of issues of race and social class.

Enlightened Racism is a major intervention into the public debate about race and perceptions of race—a debate, in the 1990s, at the heart of American political and public life. This book is indispensable to understanding that debate.

Sut Jhally and **Justin Lewis** are associate professors in the Department of Communication at the University of Massachusetts–Amherst. Both have written extensively on media and popular culture.

Index

ABC, 3
Advertising, 84, 140–141, 143–144
Affirmative action, 88–91, 128, 135–136
Amen, 102, 118, 119, 120. *See also* Black sitcoms
American dream
  and advertising, 140–141
  as myth, 7–8, 75–76, 132–133, 139
  TV promotion of, 71–75, 80–81, 88, 95, 97
  See also Class
Aronowitz, Stanley, 70
Audience ratings, 3–4, 142–144
Audience study, 8–14

Black culture, 4, 6, 11, 46, 53–54. *See also* Cultural competence
Blacks
  family life, 50, 63–64, 65
  in TV news, 60–61, 95, 114–115
  See also Blacks, class of; Blacks in TV fiction; Black sitcoms; Black viewers; Racial stereotypes; Racism
Blacks, class of, 6–7, 61–68, 62(table), 128, 132
  and class-based value system, 110, 122
  and realism of *Cosby Show,* 6–7, 81, 82
  and white viewers' obliviousness to racism, 136
  See also Blacks in TV fiction
Blacks in TV fiction, 2, 24
  black concerns, 48, 113–114, 115–116, 127, 138

class of, 35, 57–61, 59(table), 131, 132
  See also Black sitcoms; Class in TV fiction
Black sitcoms
  black viewers' attitudes toward, 50, 117–121
  and class, 78
  as stereotypical, 2, 24, 102, 103–104, 117
  white viewers' attitudes toward, 47, 101–104, 110
Black viewers
  and black sitcoms, 50, 117–121
  concern with TV images, 48, 113–114, 115–116, 127, 138
  popularity among, 48–56, 121–123, 138
  and race of Huxtables, 53–56, 134–135
  and realism, 49, 50–53, 122–128, 138
Bonet, Lisa, 22
Bourdieu, Pierre, 69
Bowles, Sam, 69
British television, 74–75
Bush, George, 62, 64–65

Capitalism, 68, 72, 74, 97, 132–133, 139, 144 *See also* Advertising
Carter, Richard, 113
Class
  culture as indicator of, 76–78, 79
  and declining significance of race, 64–68

149